WHO'S AFRAID OF THE BIG BLANK PAGE?

A lot of people are—when they realize that they have to fill that empty page with meaningful words.

Yet they shouldn't be. The simple truth is, they already have the ideas and words within them. All they have to do is find a way to ensure that their words will be *read* exactly as they were intended when they were *written*.

Now for everyone who must write to communicate—executives, students, even professional writers—Barry Tarshis provides specific guidelines for organizing ideas, creating an efficient writing environment, taking notes, developing a crack writing routine, and getting your thoughts on paper with brevity and clarity.

How To *Write* Without Pain

BARRY TARSHIS has combined his career as the highly successful author or co-author of fifteen books and numerous articles in a host of leading magazines with the acclaimed writing course he gives at seminars around the country for Fortune 500 companies. Tarshis is also a former Professor in the Graduate School of Communications at Fairfield University. His recent book *How To Write Like a Pro* is available in a Plume edition.

How
To Write
Without
Pain

BARRY TARSHIS

A PLUME BOOK

NEW AMERICAN LIBRARY

NEW YORK AND SCARBOROUGH, ONTARIO

Acknowledgements

My gratitude to the following people who, in one way or another, helped me produce this book with less pain than might otherwise have been the case: Anatole Broyard, John Boswell, David Butwin, Richard Chesnoff, Frank Deford, Stanley Englebardt, Dan Frank, Joe Esposito, John Fuller, A. E. Hotchner, Marilyn Machlowitz, Martin Marty, Pam Papay, Ray Robinson, Phyllis Robinson, Mitchell Rose, Gay Talese, Davis Weinstock, Betsy Weinstock, Mary Lou Weisman, Roger Williams, and Ken Woodward.

NAL BOOKS ARE AVAILABLE AT QUANTITY DISCOUNTS
WHEN USED TO PROMOTE PRODUCTS OR SERVICES.
FOR INFORMATION PLEASE WRITE TO PREMIUM MARKETING DIVISION,
NEW AMERICAN LIBRARY, 1633 BROADWAY, NEW YORK, NEW YORK 10019.

Copyright © 1985 by Barry Tarshis

Satellite Outline, Target Statement, ORSON, Who-Do Writing, Sign Posting, Looping Back, Umbrellaizing, and Umbrella Statement are service marks of Barry Tarshis.

Library of Congress Cataloging in Publication Data:

Tarshis, Barry.
  How to write without pain.

  1. English language—Rhetoric. I. Title.
PE1408.T336 1985   808'.042   85-2986
ISBN 0-452-25686-0

PLUME TRADEMARK REG. U.S. PAT. OFF. AND FOREIGN COUNTRIES
REG. TRADEMARK—MARCA REGISTRADA
HECHO EN HARRISONBURG, VA., U.S.A.

SIGNET, SIGNET CLASSIC, MENTOR, PLUME, MERIDIAN
and NAL BOOKS are published *in the United States*
by New American Library, 1633 Broadway, New York, New York 10019,
in Canada by The New American Library of Canada Limited,
81 Mack Avenue, Scarborough, Ontario M1L 1M8

First Printing, June, 1985

 2 3   4 5 6 7 8 9

PRINTED IN THE UNITED STATES OF AMERICA

CONTENTS

Introduction

I love being a writer.
What I can't stand is the paperwork.

—*Peter DeVries*

If you were to offer a random group of people a choice between spending an entire week at their desks doing nothing else but writing, or spending that same week in solitary confinement with nothing to eat but bread and water, more than a few of this group, I suspect, would ask you what kind of bread was being served that week in solitary confinement. The reason, of course, is that having to sit down and *write* something is not exactly everybody's idea of a day at the beach.

What is at issue here, let me point out quickly, is not so much the *inability* to write. Indeed, many people who find writing painful happen to do it exceptionally well. The issue is the degree to which so many people are obliged to suffer when they are obliged to put their thoughts down on paper. The issue is the anxiety, the frustration, and, in some instances, the agony that writing often inflicts. The issue is the inordinate amount of time and effort it often takes otherwise articulate executives to produce routine memos. The issue is the attack of hives that recently hit a student of mine as she was working on a paper that was due the next morning.

It could be argued, of course, that writing is *supposed* to be painful, that pain is the price you pay for converting the chaos inside your head to the coherency that ultimately takes shape on the printed page. Listen to novelist William Styron, who has described writing as "hell"; or the late sportswriter Red Smith, who once observed, "There is nothing to writing. All you do is sit down at a typewriter and open a vein."

Points well taken. Writing *can* be painful, and the more complicated your subject, the more deeply you need to probe your psyche for material, or the higher you set your artistic standards, the more painful it's likely to be. Freshly conceived images and ideas, precisely chosen words, artfully crafted sentence rhythms—all the qualities that are the essence of writing that engages you and absorbs you—rarely flow *naturally* from anybody's pen. And you never know, looking at the printed page of a well-written book or magazine article, how much time, effort, frustration, and turmoil was ultimately necessary to produce the finished product. As Truman Capote once put it, "Good writing is rewriting. And rewriting. And rewriting."

Fair enough. But let us not forget that most of the writing that gets churned out each day isn't really meant to be "good writing" in the classic, literary sense of the term. Most day-to-day writing doesn't usually deal with terribly complicated subjects, isn't meant to be—and shouldn't be—judged as "art," doesn't generally require you to search for skeletons in your subconscious, and, when you think about it, doesn't really require you to be inordinately original with your images and ideas, surgically precise with your wording, or lyrically artful with your sentence rhythms. Most day-to-day writing consists of business memos, letters, and reports. And while I don't want to demean the skill it takes to write these things clearly and concisely, it's worth bearing in mind the purpose behind this kind of writing: not to win literary prizes but to communicate information—information that most people could probably communicate very easily, thank you, if only they didn't have to sit down and *write* it.

What I'm saying, in other words, is that for most people who write, the process doesn't have to be—and *shouldn't* be—nearly as painful as it seems to be. And that's why I've written this book.

My premise is this: that writing is painful for so many people not because the process is inherently painful and not because the talent needed to write clearly and concisely is as rare as, say, perfect musical pitch. The reason most people find writing so painful, in my view, is that they simply *mishandle* the writing process.

You can mishandle the writing process in any number of ways. You can mishandle it by assuming that writing is something that anybody with average smarts should be able to handle off the top of his head, without having to concentrate and without having to work in an environment conducive to concentration. You can mishandle it by failing to recognize that the ultimate barometer of effectiveness in most writing situations is not how brilliantly or creatively or originally something is *written,* but how well it *reads:* how easy it is for your readers to grasp the message and the intent of your material. You can mishandle it by failing to decide, *before* you begin to commit words to paper, what you're trying to accomplish with your words, and by failing to devise an overall strategy capable of accomplishing that objective. You can mishandle it by worrying too much what specific words you use and not enough about the thoughts those words are meant to convey.

That there are so many different ways in which it is possible to mishandle the writing process is not surprising. For if you are like most people, it's unlikely that you have ever given much thought to the actual process of writing. You simply sit down and do it. Yes, you've been taught how to spell, how to punctuate, and how to put together a sentence. And, if you've taken writing courses, you've probably been taught how to organize an essay. What you are unlikely to have learned, however—because nobody is likely to have taught you—is how to put it all together, or, more to the point, how to manage the writing process more efficiently.

Which brings me again to this book and what I hope to accomplish with it. This book is *not,* let me emphasize, a book on business writing, or, for that matter, about any single type of writing. It's also not a book about how to make poems more lyrical, novels more spellbinding, or articles more saleable. Finally it warrants only marginal comparison to other books on writing—*The Elements of Style,* for instance—that deal mainly with the mechanical or stylistic aspects of writing: the words you use and the sentences you stitch together.

What the book *is* about is the writing process itself, and what I see as the very root of the writing dilemma for most people: their inability to control the mental activities that underlie the writing process. My primary objective in this book is not necessarily to make you a *better* writer (although the techniques you learn could well produce this result); it's to make you a more *efficient* writer: to help you write with less pain and difficulty than may now be the case. How do I intend to do this? By introducing you to a number of techniques whose purpose is to help you assume more control over the process itself. In brief, I want to make writing less mysterious for you, and convert what might now seem to you to be a bewildering and often intimidating process into a process that's much more logical, more purposeful, and less threatening.

The approach to writing you'll be reading about in *How to Write Without Pain* has evolved primarily from two sources: an effective writing course I taught for five years at the Fairfield University Graduate School of Corporate and Political Communication, in Fairfield, Connecticut, and writing seminars I have been conducting over the past five years for major corporations throughout the United States. Most of the students in these courses are not professional writers, but businesspeople, sales and technical professionals, and teachers—people who write not out of choice but out of necessity, people who are looking for one thing, above all: to be able to *use* the writing process more effectively on the job or in school. It's safe to say, I think, that most of the people who've taken my courses have been greatly helped by what they've learned, and they are now able to put their thoughts on paper with considerably less pain—and with better results—than was once the case.

I can't promise that the concepts and techniques you will read about in *How to Write Without Pain* will take *all* of the mystery out of writing or eliminate *all* of the difficulty you experience when you write. Still, I think you will find this book of great *practical* value in your day-to-day writing. You'll learn how to adopt a mental approach to writing that doesn't sabotage your efforts before you've even picked up a pencil or stationed yourself at your typewriter. You'll learn how to create a more efficient writing environment and how to follow a more efficient writing routine. And, most important, you'll learn a number of specific techniques that should enable you, once and for all, to handle your day-to-day writing with more confidence and less anguish.

1 | Why It Hurts

Imagine for a moment what it would be like to drive a car in which the gas pedal, the clutch, and the brake pedal were constantly changing positions so that you never knew until you actually pushed down one of the pedals whether the car was going to go faster, slow down, or do nothing at all.

Now imagine that you've been asked to drive this car, its unpredictability notwithstanding, to somewhere you've never been, and that you've been given only the vaguest of directions. Imagine, too, that you have no choice in this matter: you *must* get to your destination and you must be there within, say, an hour. One more thing while we're at it: imagine that the route you have been asked to take includes a lengthy stretch on your city's busiest freeway—at the peak of the rush hour.

I have asked you to imagine all of this, as you might suspect, for a reason that relates very much to writing. For driving an unpredictable car to an unfamiliar destination amid a variety of pressures is not unlike the situation that confronts you whenever you sit down to write.

Think about it a minute. Writing obliges you to use a vehicle—your mind—that doesn't necessarily move where and when you want it to move. Writing frequently takes you into areas that you know little or nothing about. And writing, particularly the kind of writing you do for work or for school, almost invariably embodies some element of pressure, whether it's a tight deadline or a hostile army of people who must read and pass judgment on what you've written.

If I seem to be stretching the metaphor here, forgive me. But writing doesn't lend itself to conventional analysis. Nobody really knows, after all, what has to happen inside the brain to produce writing. Nobody knows how thoughts are generated, how thoughts give rise to the words that express these thoughts, what mechanisms are at work when a writer decides that one word works better than another in a particular situation, or what specific mental processes are activated when we are shaping words into sentences, linking sentences into paragraphs, or revising what we've already written.

Not only does nobody *know* much about any of this internal business, but until recently nobody seemed much interested in the subject, never mind that writing is an almost universal activity that's been part of the human experience for seven thousand years. Because writing isn't really *behavioral*—you can't *observe* what's going on in people's minds as they write— experimental psychologists have long ignored it. And linguists and English scholars, too, have tended to ignore the process aspect of writing because it was—well, too mundane. Better to explore the symbolic implications of *Beowulf* than to stoop to conquer the nuts and bolts of sentence structure.

Happily, though, this neglectful picture is changing, thanks to the emergence in recent years of a new science known as cognitive psychology, which might best be described as the science of the mind. Unlike their colleagues in other branches of psychology, cognitive psychologists don't really care that you can't directly observe what happens inside the mind, they're interested, anyway; and a growing number of cognitive psychologists have been looking specifically at writing, trying to develop a picture of the mental dynamics that underlie it. Admittedly, no one as yet has come close to solving the mystery of how writing actually happens, but we know more about the mental dynamics of writing today than we used to know, and, more important, we can now begin to develop some approaches to writing that are related, in a general way at least, to these dynamics.

What Really Happens When We Write?

Perhaps the most important insight to emerge out of all the various writing studies that have been reported over the past decade is that when you come right down to it, there may not even *be* such a thing as writing—at least not as we normally perceive the term.

Let me explain. Not very long ago, writing—and let's define writing for now as the process of expressing thoughts on paper with the idea of communicating these thoughts to a reader—was seen as a *single* cognitive function, something for which you either had or didn't have a "flair." It is now clear, of course, that writing is *not* a single cognitive function but a smorgasbord of cognitive activities that range from many of the same general mental skills you use routinely in other areas of your life, such as analyzing situations, setting up a general plan, and organizing your thoughts, to highly specific skills (punctuation, for example) that are of no use to you *except* when you're writing.

Exactly how *many* different cognitive functions play a part in writing is difficult to say since the number will vary according to the nature and the complexity of the writing task. If you're writing a novel, for instance, there are any number of considerations—plot, character development, pacing, etc.—that won't concern you if you're writing a technical report. But even relatively simple writing tasks embody more decision making than most people realize, obliging you to decide, among other things, what thoughts to express, what words to use to express those thoughts, what tone to strike, and how long—or short—to make your sentences or paragraphs. Which isn't to mention the more prosaic decisions involving spelling, punctuation, and grammar.

But the problem isn't so much the *number* of cognitive functions that writing embodies. It's the fact that when you write you are expected to execute most of these cognitive functions at more or less the same time. As psychologist Richard Hayes of Carnegie-Mellon University explains it, writing is not a purely linear process, and what writers do should not be compared to what cooks do when they bake cakes or what CPAs do when they prepare income-tax returns. "Writers," points out Hayes, "are more like busy switchboard operators trying to juggle a number of demands on their attention and constraints on their time."

I would like you to focus for a moment or two on this image—your brain having to "juggle" a number of functions at one time—for it represents the rationale behind most of the concepts and techniques I'm going to be talking about throughout this book. Like Hayes, I contend that much of the pain and difficulty that writing produces can be traced to the fact that the brain, remarkable though its powers may be, doesn't do terribly well when it's called upon to focus actively on more than one thing at a time, which is precisely what the brain is called upon to do when we write.

This not to say, of course, that the brain is *incapable* of handling several mental tasks at the same time, only that it can do so efficiently when the majority of the tasks at hand require little or no *conscious* decision making. Whenever you drive a car, for instance, you don't *consciously* think about how much pressure you need to exert on the gas pedal or how far to the right or left you need to turn the steering wheel to execute a turn: all that information gets processed more or less automatically, through something often referred to as "muscle memory."

Ideally, the same principle should apply to writing, the difference being, however, that except for the most basic elements of writing—spelling, punctuation, grammar, etc.—the process

doesn't readily lend itself to automation. Yes, it's possible to reduce the number of cognitive demands your brain must attend
to simultaneously when you write, but to do so you need to understand, first of all, the different *kinds* of cognitive decisions
that writing calls for and, secondly, you need to organize the
process so that the decisions come in a reasonably logical sequence.

To be sure, I am simplifying an extremely complex set of
events, and I haven't even mentioned some of the other considerations that further complicate matters: the fact that our
brains have a built-in tendency to drift, rather than focus on
one thing (which explains why it's so difficult to concentrate on
one thing for any length of time); the fact that our ability to *generate* thoughts far outpaces our ability to put these thoughts
down on paper (which explains why we frequently ''forget''
what we want to write before we've had a chance to write it
down); the fact that much of what happens when we write is *beyond* our conscious control, a dilemma I'll explore in a later
chapter.

Then again, I don't want to paint too bleak a picture of what
you have to contend with when you write at this early stage of
the book and, above all, I don't want to get bogged down in
theory. Yes, writing is difficult, and yes, we haven't as yet
evolved a network of neural circuitry sophisticated enough to
meet its cognitive demands with any true degree of efficiency.
But this is not to say that you can't learn to manage the process
far more efficiently than you are now managing it. So while it's
important, certainly, that you understand *why* writing is difficult, it's more important that you start to learn some specific
strategies for easing this pain and difficulty. And here, in short,
is the challenge that will occupy us throughout the rest of the
book.

2 | How to Get Out of Your Own Way

Whatever difficulties writing may embody in and of itself, and whatever pressures may come to bear upon your own particular writing tasks, it's a safe bet that a prime source of your difficulty is you yourself. Indeed, out of the hundreds of people I've worked with in my courses, I've yet to meet anybody (and I include myself in this category, by the way) who didn't contribute in one way or another to his or her own writing misery.

So before we begin looking at specific techniques designed to help you write more easily, I'd like to address two aspects of writing that, on the one hand, have nothing to do with the skills necessary to manage the process more efficiently, but on the other hand, affect profoundly your ability to *use* these skills to strategic advantage. I'm talking, first of all, about the attitudes you bring to writing, and secondly, about the conditions in which you write.

In this chapter, we'll look at how the way you *feel* about writing can affect how easily it comes for you. In Chapter 3, we'll look at how the routine you follow (or don't follow) and the conditions in which you write can either enhance or impede your writing efficiency.

The Power of Mental Sets

In a series of experiments conducted in the early 1960s, a group of college students were handed two small birthday candles, a box of matches, and a few thumbtacks, and were asked to figure out a way to mount the two candles on the wall. The same problem was presented to a second group, the only difference being that the students in this group were told that if they solved the problem within a certain time frame, they would win a twenty-dollar reward. Both groups figured the answer out eventually (the solution, if you're wondering, is to empty the box, tack it to the wall, and then place the candles on it), but it took the group expecting the reward *more* time to solve the problem than the other group.

The term psychologists use to describe this phenomenon is *mental set*. The idea is that we often have more than enough basic skills or knowledge to solve a certain problem, yet falter because of mental attitude: we either don't care *enough* or, more often, care *too much* about the outcome.

Mental set is the reason athletes sometimes "choke" in pressure situations, and although choking is not a phenomenon you normally associate with writing, I can assure you that it's just as likely to happen at your writing desk as it is on a tennis court or a golf course. It simply has a different name. It's called "writer's block."

I'll have more to say about writer's block in Chapter 11. For now, though, let me stress that just about everybody who writes experiences blocking to some degree—I've sometimes brooded for hours in front of a typewriter without turning out a single acceptable sentence—and there is no single way to prevent it from occurring or to snap out of it when it strikes. Probably the only *true* antidote to blocking—if there is such a true antidoce—is confidence, but the only way you can develop confidence, if I can be excused for belaboring the obvious, is to build up a solid record of accomplishment. (Even then your confidence can crumble on you at any moment. You would be amazed at how *little* confidence in their writing ability you find even among writers with established reputations. I can remember years ago hearing the well-respected novelist Richard Yates lament that 90 percent of the time he was working on his first novel, *Revolutionary Road,* he was convinced he was turning out "drivel.")

But if I can't give you a surefire technique for conquering writer's block, I can talk briefly about some of the specific mental sets that can contribute to it and offer some suggestions on how to change these sets.

Love Me, Love My Writing

Occasionally in my seminars, I run into people (usually they are scientists or technicians) to whom pride of authorship is an alien concept. They see writing as nothing more than slapping down on paper whatever comes into their heads. They couldn't care less about what you or anybody else might think about *how* these thoughts are expressed.

Not surprisingly, the writing produced by such people is generally unreadable, and so I would hardly advocate so cavalier a philosophy. I will say this, however: people who don't care beans about their reputations as writers write with little or no pain, and I can think of any number of my students who would do well to adopt at least a smidgen of this same philosophy. I'm talking here about people whose pride of authorship is *excessive,* and whose chief concern when they write is not necessarily to communicate information but to make darn sure that you take notice of their writing brilliance.

All things considered, it's no wonder that so many people should feel compelled to impress you when they write. Most of the writing we do in school, after all, is meant to prove to our teachers with how "well" or "creatively" we do it. That's okay up to a point, but once you leave school, most people who read what you write are not terribly interested in how "good" or "creative" a writer you are: that's *your* business. What readers are interested in most of the time—particularly readers of business correspondence—is being able to read and to understand the information you are communicating as quickly and as easily as possible. Indeed, about the only time most people are likely to take notice of your writing is when the information isn't being conveyed clearly or concisely enough. As I preach over and over to my students, nobody takes home memos or reports to read by the fire.

I'm not suggesting that it's unhealthy to take pride in the way you write. Nor am I "anti-style" as one former student implied when he asked what I had against "well-turned" phrases. The fact is, I have nothing against well-turned phrases. I enjoy reading them, and I enjoy writing them. I just don't happen to think there's much of a call for well-turned phrases in most day-to-day business correspondence or, for that matter, in most school papers. If I'm a busy executive with more reading than I can comfortably handle as it is, I'm not looking for poetic flourishes or zippy one-liners in the memos I read, and I'm not interested in how creative or clever the writer is. If I want clever, I'll read Woody Allen.

The point is this: pride of authorship is fine, and it's important certainly to your business career or your academic record that you demonstrate to your superiors or your teachers that you can express your ideas on paper clearly and concisely. But once your impulse to dazzle people with your verbal footwork gets out of hand, it becomes an albatross—for you and for the people who have to read what you write.

So let me offer a suggestion that might spare you some effort and embarrassment. If, as you're writing, you begin to hear in the back of your mind some powerful musical theme—the final movement of Beethoven's Ninth, perhaps—chances are you're getting too swept up by how you're trying to *sound*. If you are writing to please yourself, fine. Enjoy. If, however, you're writing to communicate information, a little easier on the crescendos, please. Just deliver your information as naturally as

you can without all the fanfare. You'll be surprised at how
much easier the process will become for you. You may be surprised, too, by the number of people who start telling you how
well you do it.

The Talent Factor

That there is a component of talent to writing—and
let's define *talent* as a difficult-to-isolate mix of writing-related
cognitive capacities that are largely inborn, and leave it at
that—is all but indisputable. How else to explain Shakespeare,
Keats, or Joyce?

The relevant question, though, isn't whether there *is* such a
thing as writing "talent" but how necessary that talent is to the
kind of writing most people do daily—namely business reports,
memos, and school papers.

As I suggested in the Introduction, I myself don't happen to
think talent terribly essential to these enterprises (helpful, perhaps, but certainly not vital), but quite a few people I know do
not share my viewpoint. More people than you might imagine
have convinced themselves that they will never write *anything*
easily because they weren't really "born" to do so.

The impact that such a perception can have on your writing
fluency requires little elaboration. If you are convinced that
you do not write easily because you were not issued the genes
that underlie this rare talent, you are unlikely to approach the
process in a workmanlike, problem-solving manner. You will
also procrastinate more than most people do, and, when you
get bogged down, you will be more likely than most people to
head for the nearest coffee station or water cooler. My guess,
too, is that you will do everything in your power to *avoid* writing. After all, if God had intended you to write well, He would
have endowed you with the "talent."

I can probably explain my position better by talking for a
moment about the talent you need—or don't need—to drive a
car. Few of us were born with the reflexes needed to compete

in, say, the Indianapolis 500, but the reflexes most of us were born with are certainly serviceable enough that we can drive our cars pretty much where we want to drive them.

Similarly, few of us were endowed with whatever literary gifts are necessary to produce a *Ulysses* or a *Catcher in the Rye* or a "Love Song of J. Alfred Prufrock," but so what? Such talent is not only superfluous to the writing tasks most people do on a day-to-day basis, it could well interfere. I know successful novelists who become all thumbs when they have to write a simple letter, and I know celebrated journalists who couldn't write a press release if their lives depended upon it: they would invariably try to turn it into an *Esquire* cover story.

I'm not minimizing the value of talent; nor am I deprecating the challenges of day-to-day report, memo, or term-paper writing. I'm simply saying that to turn out readable memos and reports and quality term papers, you don't have to be an Indy-car-driver of a writer. More to the point, you don't have to bring a crash helmet to your writing desk.

Writing "By the Book"

I once had a seminar participant, an eighteen-year-old college student, walk out of one of my sessions in a cold sweat. I was discussing a topic I refer to as "personalizing" and was trying to demonstrate how much more smoothly and more invitingly a passage reads if, instead of writing, "The system has been designed to help each individual in our organization do his or her job more efficiently," you write, "The system has been designed to help you do your job more efficiently." Said the girl on her way out: "If I ever wrote the word 'you' in one of my English papers, I'd get an F."

She was probably right. More often than not, the writing suggestions I gave to my son when he was in high school were rejected because his teacher, he told me, would find them too ungrammatical, too idiomatic, or too who knows what else.

All of this is terribly unfortunate—unfortunate because most of the "formal" writing training we receive in high school and college doesn't adequately prepare us for the kind of writing we do once we stop writing for grades and begin to write to communicate. Worse, much of this "training" can actually interfere with your ability to communicate.

To illustrate my point, I'd like you to think for a moment about something you know how to do very well, whether it's hitting a tennis ball, preparing pasta primavera, or changing the tire on a car. Once you've come up with a subject, pretend there's somebody in the room with you, and try to explain to this imaginary person how to do this particular thing you know how to do well, albeit with one condition: that you bear in mind, *as* you are talking, some of the principles of "correct" writing you were taught in school. I don't want you to use the personal pronouns "I" or "you," for instance. I don't want you to use any contractions. I don't want you to repeat any words (use synonyms instead). And I don't you to begin any sentences with "and" or "but," or end any of your sentences with prepositions.

Unless you're unusual, you're going to find yourself somewhat tongue-tied early on in your presentation. And no wonder. As soon you ask your brain to do one thing while it's concentrating on what it *shouldn't* be doing, you create the one condition the brain is least equipped to handle: conflict.

Mind you, I am not railing against the conventions of proper grammar, and I'm not suggesting that you shouldn't be concerned with whether you've used the correct tense or placed your commas where commas are supposed to be placed. I'm simply cautioning you against being overly *consumed* by these considerations *as* you are putting your thoughts into words. And I'm cautioning you, in particular, against being overly consumed by "rules" that may no longer be relevant or productive in your particular writing situation. Granted, if your grammar is shaky, you'll have to smooth out the rough edges of your prose at some point in the process (and if you're worried about your grammar, incidentally, it's not a bad idea to get hold of a book on grammar and teach yourself the basics). And if you have a teacher or else work for somebody who insists that you write in his or her style, you have little choice but to go along with the program, my advice notwithstanding.

On the other hand, keep in mind what it does to your writing efficiency each time you throw your already overburdened brain an additional mental set to juggle. At the very least, no matter what mental sets you take with you to your writing table, try to compartmentalize them and do your best to keep them from impeding you during the *early* stages of writing, when the thrust of your mental energy should be on clarifying your ideas and getting them down in rough form. If you do nothing else I suggest in this book, in fact, but eliminate disruptive mental sets from your overall approach to writing (and eliminate, in particular, those discussed in this chapter), you're likely to see an almost immediate improvement not only in your writing efficiency but in the quality of the finished product as well.

3 | Creating the Right Conditions

I can't think of any skill-dependent activity—whether it's hitting a tennis ball, cooking a soufflé, or singing the title role in *Rigoletto*—in which the quality of performance isn't influenced by the conditions under which you are obliged to perform.

Writing, of course, is no exception, and yet I am forever running into people who act as if writing *were* an exception to this rule and who consistently—and stubbornly—write under conditions that would sabotage even the most skillful writers. If I were asked to name the one thing in fact that most differentiates professional writers from people who write as part of their jobs, it would be that professionals pay noticeably more attention to the routines they follow and are oh so much fussier about the environments in which they write.

True, professional writers usually have an edge over nonprofessionals in that they usually write in environments of their own choosing and are usually in a better position than students or businesspeople to organize their daily schedules *around* their writing. But these advantages don't diminish the practical importance of the principle: the more regular your writing routine and the more conducive to writing you can make your surroundings, the easier it is going to be for you to handle the demands of the writing process. Let's look now at some of the practical aspects of this principle.

Setting Aside the Time

I wish it were otherwise, but writing requires intense concentration, and no matter how accomplished a writer you become, you can't expect to do your best unless you can set aside blocks of time in which you can focus exclusively on the writing and not have to contend with frequent interruptions.

This is not always an easy principle to follow, I know, particularly if you have one of those jobs in which you are forever being called upon to put out fires, or, if you work in a chummy office, where colleagues are forever poking their heads inside your doorway to find out if you watched *Hill Street Blues* the night before or if you feel up to Mexican food for lunch.

Still, I've found that the majority of people who maintain they *can't* insulate themselves from interruptions when they write at work are people who have never really *tried* to do so. Sometimes, oddly enough, it's never *occurred* to them to do so: they simply don't accord to writing the importance they give to other aspects of their jobs. But sometimes, too, they don't *want* to do it: they simply don't cotton well to being alone in a room with nothing for company but a pad and a pencil; they'd rather be splashing around in the middle of the office swim.

Foolish thinking, to my mind, and for obvious reasons. Except in those rare instances when the document you're writing requires almost no thought—an agenda for a meeting, for instance—writing isn't like knitting a sweater: you can't keep putting it aside and picking it up again where you left off. It takes time to build up a head of mental steam, and it doesn't take much in the way of a distraction—a phone call that lasts all of thirty seconds could easily do it—for whatever head of mental steam you've built up to evaporate. So, unless you're an exception, you'll get more writing done in an hour of uninterrupted time than you're likely to get done in four or five hours of intermittent writing punctuated by frequent interruptions, even though the interruptions themselves, when you add them all up, might not amount to more than fifteen or twenty minutes.

The *length* of time you set aside for your writing—and how you schedule that time—will depend, naturally, upon the nature of your job and the role that writing plays in it. If writing is simply one of many things you do in your job, it's probably impractical to think in terms of an entire morning or afternoon devoted to nothing but your writing. But if you're not already doing so, I would urge you to set aside specific blocks of writing time during the week, making sure you give yourself at least an hour each time. You need at least an hour, I think, to get into any sort of productive writing rhythm. I also think you're better off (given a choice) scheduling your writing hours on a reasonably spread out basis rather than allowing your writing chores to pile up until you have no choice but to grind them out in one marathon session. Some people, I grant you, *need* a certain amount of pressure in order to get their writing tasks accomplished, and you may be one such person. But whatever advantages that extra jolt of adrenalin might produce in the short term are more than offset, I think, by the disruption and the anguish that marathon writing sessions can produce. By writing a little every day, you help end the vicious cycle of putting off the writing until it piles up, suffering when you have to grind it out under pressure, and then, bearing in mind the suffering, putting it off again the next time.

While you're at it, you might try to schedule your writing time at more or less the same hour each day. Just as athletes usually perform better when they routinize their training schedule, so, I think, do writers operate more efficiently when there is a uniformity (within reason) to their writing schedules. Most professionals work best in the morning, among them John Fuller, who averages a book a year and has disciplined himself to wake up each morning at four A.M. so that he can be at his typewriter—or, as he puts it, so he can "catch" his type-writer—no later than 4:45 A.M. "I'm not crazy about the schedule," he admits. "But it's the only way I can get the work done."

I'm not suggesting, heaven help us, that *you* start waking up at four o'clock in the morning, the better to handle your daily writing tasks, but I don't want to mislead you, either. As I said earlier, regardless of how accomplished a writing technician you become, you'll never be to take writing for granted. It will always require concentration. And time. Conceivably, you may have no choice: your job may be such that you *must* write in bits and pieces. If so, you have my sympathies. I would urge you, however, not to give up too soon in your attempt to *find* time to set aside.

Look at it this way. If you're already spending, say, ten to fifteen hours a month writing in a hit-or-miss, bits and pieces fashion, it's possible that a more disciplined writing schedule could cut that total in half. So what I'm suggesting, finally, is that by setting aside time for your writing, you'll probably end up with *more* time to attend to your other responsibilities, not less. Some suggestions:

- On days when you're going to be writing, wake up forty-five minutes earlier and spend the first forty-five minutes of your day working on the writing.
- If there are too many distractions where you normally work, go someplace more private (if you can), like a conference room or library.
- Put a Do Not Disturb sign on your office door (if you have a door) and, if possible, put a hold on all phone calls.
- Try to educate the people around you and who work for you to respect your need for uninterrupted time.

Creating the "Right" Writing Environment

For eleven years, Martin Marty, the remarkably prolific and versatile writer who heads the Divinity School at the University of Chicago, did much of his writing during the summer on a small island in the lake country north of Chicago. The lake house had two decks, one on each side of the house, and the only difference between the two, apart from a slightly different view, was that one was a little smaller. Even so, says Marty, he found that he could do his writing on only the larger deck. If he had to move his writing table to the smaller deck—when there were children playing on the larger deck, for instance—he might as well have been in the lake itself. "I simply couldn't think straight on that second deck," he says. "To this day, I can't explain why."

Why so slight a change in surroundings could so stifle a normally prolific writer is something I'm not sure I can explain, either, particularly since I know a number of successful professional writers who, unlike Marty, seem impervious to their surroundings and who, if pressed, could probably set up a writing table in the middle of Grand Central Station. Ray Robinson, the executive editor of *Seventeen* magazine, says he can write on a crowded bus. Marilyn Machlowitz, a psychologist whose books include *Workaholics,* wrote the bulk of her doctoral dissertation at Yale on the train between New York and New Haven. And when novelist and playwright David Wiltse moved his writing office from a small studio to an upstairs bedroom in another house, it took him, he said, all of an hour to get used to the change. "Once you're into your writing," he says, "it doesn't really matter where you are."

Maybe so. But the majority of writers I know have more in common with Martin Marty than with Ray Robinson, Marilyn

Machlowitz, and David Wiltse, and I am no exception. Whenever I am obliged to write in surroundings other than my office, I am not only less productive, I become edgy and cranky. My mind, unlike my stomach, doesn't travel well.

Conceivably we could be dealing here with nothing more complicated than self-indulgence, and it could well be that if the less adaptive among us were *forced* to write in unfamiliar surroundings, we could eventually adjust.

Fine, but even if we could adjust, it would take time and, more important, it would probably be painful. And that's really the point. Not that you *can't* overcome the distractions in your surroundings, only that to do so usually takes extra effort and concentration—effort and concentration that would be more wisely invested in your writing.

What sort of environment is the *most* conducive to writing? How much space should you have? What should the view (if any) be like? What kind of music should you listen to: Mozart? James Taylor? Pavarotti? Michael Jackson? Or none?

These are all logical questions, and I wish I could supply some logical answers. When it comes to the most productive environment, however, no two writers I know are alike. Some professional writers like to work in big rooms so they can pace back and forth the way you see screen-writers do in movies about Hollywood. Others prefer the womblike confinement of very small rooms. Some writers are comfortable with clutter, others need order. One writer I know can't work well in a room that doesn't have an abundance of natural light. Another writer I know likes the room to be dark except for her writing table. Woody Allen says he'd rather write in his bedroom than anyplace else and can't understand how anybody could write and listen to music at the same time. Gay Talese, who admits that he has spent more money than he cares to think about trying to create the "perfect" writing environment, does most of his writing in a windowless studio (albeit an attractive one) two stories below street level. One writer I know refuses to put *anything* on the walls of her office; another has his room ringed with framed reprints of his best articles. "I need them," he says, "for inspiration."

I don't mean to imply that the solution to your writing problems may lie in finding the right interior decorator, and I'm aware, too, you may not have the luxury of being able to tailor your writing environment to your own psychological specifications. On the other hand, regardless of *where* you work, there are a few critical aspects of your writing environment that you *can*—and *should*—assume control over in the interests of writing efficiency.

To begin with, whether you work at home or in an office, you should designate a special room—or, if you can't set aside a room, a certain corner in a room or office—as your writing "place." How cluttered or neat you want to keep this place, how many, or few, books you want to be surrounded by, what you want—or don't want—to see hanging on the walls, what you want your gaze to dwell upon whenever you look up from your typewriter, pad, or computer—that's all up to you. What's important is that you're able to get started as soon as you sit down. This means that your writing tools (typewriter, pencils, pad, etc.) are easily accessible, that you have enough space to spread out whatever notes you've gathered and that, if need be, you're in arm's reach of a dictionary, file cabinet, or whatever else you might need to get your hands on as you're writing.

Don't ignore the purely physical aspects of the place—how hot or cold it gets (for the record, our brains operate most effectively at a temperature of about sixty-five degrees Fahrenheit) and how good the light is. Natural light is healthier than artificial light, but you don't want to sit in direct sunlight. And if you work in a room with a window, think twice before setting up your writing table directly in front of the window, regardless of the view (and maybe because of the view). It isn't only that the activity outside the window could be distracting, it's that working in front of a window forces your eyes to adjust to the change of light each time you look up and down, so they will fatigue more quickly.

Give some thought to the chair you use when you write. Ideally, it should be both comfortable *and* supportive—a combination, alas, that could prove as difficult to find as a plumber who comes when he says he's coming and doesn't charge you an arm and a leg. Most really *comfortable* chairs—the chairs you like to curl up in when you're reading or watching television—can be murder on your back if you try to sit in them for any length of time when you write. This means that if you're looking for support as well as comfort, you'll probably end up with a chair that looks like something out of *Star Wars* and you'll end up spending a lot more money than you figure a chair is worth. Bite the bullet, anyway—particularly if you spend more than two or three hours a day writing. The money you save on orthopedic bills will more than cover the investment.

The size of your desk or writing table is worth thinking about, too, assuming you have options. Because I often work on projects in which there is an unwieldy mass of data, I like to have plenty of space. That way I can spread out all the papers, as if I were General Patton in a war room. I also prefer a reverse L-shaped arrangement, my writing table jutting out to the right of a long counter. This arrangement enables me to have everything I need—notes, reference books, paper—within arm's reach.

Now let's talk finally about noise or, better still, the absence of it. Most people prefer it fairly quiet when they write, but newspaper people and radio and television newswriters have learned to concentrate in less than monastic silence, and I, for one, get a little spooked when it's *too* quiet. The issue isn't so much the level of the noise, but what you become accustomed to—a principle, of course, that holds true to your surroundings in general. The more intensely you have to concentrate when you write, the more vulnerable you are to distractions and the more important it becomes to work in surroundings that are uniform, predictable, and, above all, work for *you*. As Karin

Mack and Eric Skjei point out in *Overcoming Writing Blocks* (J. P. Tarcher, 1979), by setting up an environment that offers you the optimum balance of comfort, convenience, and privacy (all within reason, of course), you set into motion a process that also helps you to take charge of yourself and your writing. "Just the simple feeling that you're actively molding your surroundings," say Mack and Skjei, "will dispel the helpless feeling that being blocked brings and will carry on into the writing process as well."

Tools of the Trade

Since some of the greatest works of literature were written with some of the crudest writing implements imaginable, it could be argued that the particular tool you choose to write with—whether it be pen, pencil, typewriter, or word processor—has little or no bearing on the outcome of the writing effort.

True enough. But a growing body of evidence suggests that the method you use to produce your writing may have more bearing on the difficulty writing presents for you than you might think. If the method itself is demanding enough (as is the case with young children who haven't yet mastered penmanship), the attention the method requires could divert mental energy from the higher-level challenges of writing, and with predictably frustrating results.

Just how *much* of a difference your method of putting the words to paper can make in your overall writing fluency is difficult to say, for it will largely depend on the nature of your day-to-day writing tasks (and especially on the amount of revising you have to do) and what you've become accustomed to. But let's look at some of the options.

Longhand Versus Typing

If you're a reasonably good typist (i.e., if you can type at least forty words per minute) and have learned how to "think" on the typewriter (no mean achievement, by the way), it's probably more efficient to type than it is to write longhand. Typing is faster and not as physically demanding as writing longhand (fewer people complain of "typist's cramp" than they do of "writer's cramp"). What's more, a typed manuscript is easier to read, edit, and revise than a handwritten manuscript, especially if you have a handwriting like mine.

But writing longhand has it advantages, too. If you write longhand, you can do your writing almost anywhere, and you never have to concern yourself with mechanical glitches—ribbons to change, keys sticking, the power going out—or any of the other mechanical hazards, however minor, that come with the territory when you type.

Interestingly, many professional writers who can both type well and think on the typewriter nonetheless choose to write longhand, a fact that suggests two possibilities: one, regardless of how well you type, the mechanical demands of typing still interfere to some extent with your concentration; two, for certain people, certain types of writing—poetry, for instance, or any other writing in which you are reaching deep inside yourself for ideas—lend themselves better to longhand, which is, you might say, the "purest" medium. Anatole Broyard says he finds writing with a pencil and pad more "intimate" than sitting in front of a machine. And Betsy Weinstock, a staff writer for *The New Yorker,* describes the difference between the two as being one of "immediacy." "Writing with longhand," she says, "is simply more *personal.*"

Not that you have to choose one over the other in all situations. A. E. Hotchner, best known for his biography of Ernest Hemingway, prefers to write his first drafts in longhand and to type subsequent drafts, and he reports that Hemingway liked to switch back and forth depending on the kind of passage he was working on, typing dialogue and writing description in longhand. Gay Talese, too, moves back and forth between writing and typing, depending on the difficulty he's having getting his ideas on paper.

All things considered, I think typing is a far more efficient and less arduous way of generating writing than writing longhand, particularly when it comes to routine business correspondence, and I would urge you, if you're young and you have the time, to learn how to type and, more important, to learn how to compose *directly* on the typewriter. It may not be that easy for you to make the conversion from longhand to typewriter—you need to do it gradually—but most people who've made the switch would agree, I think, that the initial struggle is worth that long-term payoff, especially when you consider that being able to type has become a prerequisite for working on a word processor. But more of word processing later.

Speaking It Out

The conventional view of dictating your thoughts, as opposed to writing them down, is that dictation is certainly a faster method of getting thoughts down on paper but takes a long time to learn and lends itself only to certain types of writing tasks, namely routine letters or memos.

There is, however, at least one researcher—John D. Gould, who works for IBM at the T. J. Watson Research Center—who thinks otherwise. Gould has run studies in which college students have become reasonably proficient at dictating after only a day's practice, and Gould believes that the only reason most people don't dictate more efficiently is that they don't do it enough.

Gould's results need clarification. To begin with, the speed advantage of dictating—and Gould figures that most people can dictate about 2.5 times faster than they can type—doesn't take into consideration "planning time," which, for the most part, stays the same regardless of the writing method you use.

Neither do his results take into account the time it takes for somebody else to type what you've dictated. It's important to mention, too, that the barometer Gould used for "effectiveness" in his study wasn't how *well* a piece of writing was written, but how well it *communicated*. I mention this only because, for better or worse, high school and college teachers tend to be a lot fussier about syntax than businesspeople.

All the same, my own experience with dictating, along with what I've been able to learn from others who dictate regularly, pretty much corroborates Gould's findings. It took me less time than I would have thought, for instance, to learn how to dictate simple and even slightly complex one- and two-page letters, and I don't think the letters I compose on my word processor, while they may read a little more smoothly, are *measurably* better than those I dictate.

This is not to say I would attempt to dictate a manuscript as complex as the manuscript of this book, although I know of some writers who do, in fact, dictate drafts from their notes. My suspicion is that these people spend more time *away* from the typewriter planning and thinking than I do, and they probably have a better memory than I have. In most instances, I need to *see,* not only hear, what I've written if I'm to feel comfortable about where I'm going next.

To summarize, then, you can probably improve your proficiency at dictating by doing it more often, but you still need to have a clear idea in your mind of what you want to say *before* you begin to dictate. All told, the prime advantage of dictating is that it's the only method that allows you to do something else (ride an exercise bike or drive a car) while you're actually putting your thoughts into words.

Word Processors: Should You or Shouldn't You?

Let's begin with the disadvantages.

The chief disadvantage of a word processor, to my mind, is the price. Even though the cost of word processors has been dropping steadily, you still have to spend over $1,000 for a basic system with a printer (a machine that will convert the words you typed into the screen onto paper), and more if you want expanded text management features or a reasonably fast printer that will give you "letter quality" text instead of the dots you get from the so-called dot matrix printers.

Your expenses, moreover, do not stop with the initial purchase. Diskettes—the round gizmos on which you store your your data—run five or six dollars apiece, and the ribbons and paper needed for a printer are two to three times as expensive as the ribbons and the paper needed for a typewriter. Should something go wrong with your processor, moreover, the repair expenses can be chilling. The repair service I use, for example, charges $85 an hour, starting from the moment the repairman (excuse me, "technician") leaves his office, which is a good half-hour from where I live. This means it costs me $170 for travel expenses alone and explains why I have no choice but to buy a yearly maintenance contract, which runs close to $100 a month. You can buy a lot of pens and pencils for $100 a month.

There are other disadvantages as well. Depending upon the system you buy, and how familiar you are with computers, it's going to take you anywhere from a week to a month to become comfortable with the thing. It isn't that processors are so complicated to run—they simply work on their own logic, that's all. I have a key on my processor, for instance, that reads DEL, which I refer to as my delete key, except that it doesn't *delete* anything: it serves a different function altogether. If I want to delete something, I have to press the CTRL (control) key and another key, depending on what I want to delete: a word, a paragraph, a sentence. What's worse, though, is that once you do become accustomed to working with a word processor, it's very difficult—at least it's been that way for me—to go back to straight typing, let alone longhand.

Not to mention the unsettling possibility that either through the errant push of the wrong key or some other act of man or God, you can inadvertently lose or destroy the better part of a day's—or even week's—work. Most systems have built-in controls designed to minimize this sort of thing, but the controls aren't built into the person who *runs* the machine. Only recently, while I was clearing some papers from my desk, I bent—and ruined—a floppy diskette, and because I had failed to "back up" (i.e., copy to another diskette) the material on the diskette, I lost a good day's work. It could have been worse. It could have been a diskette on which I'd stored a month's work, so it was a good lesson. I now back up my diskettes as religiously as I brush my teeth. Sometimes.

Having spelled out the liabilities of word processing, let me now say that I find the system I use all but indispensable.

Its prime virtue (and the virtue that, to my mind, outweighs all the liabilities combined) is the drudgery it eliminates when you're revising what you've already written. True, if the first draft you produce is very close to the finished product (close enough that you can get by with pencil editings), the revising capability of a processor is probably of limited value, and buying a word processor would be tantamount to buying a new Porsche to ferry you to and from the train station.

But if you usually write several drafts of a document, each draft producing a higher degree of polish, and if you are one of those writers, like I used to be, who is forever starting paragraphs on fresh sheets of paper and then scrunching up those sheets of paper and throwing them away, word processing is just about the most wonderful thing that has ever come down the pike. Once you've typed your first draft into a word processor, you see, you never have to *retype* on subsequent drafts any material that stays the same. You change only the words and sentences you want to change and, once you've mastered a few key strokes, you do it easily and quickly. When you want to see the new draft, you let the printer do the retyping while you sip coffee, do sit-ups, or work on your tan.

The practical significance of all these revision capabilities, at least where I am concerned, is monumental. Before I got my processor, I probably spent a good 70 to 80 percent of my writing time simply *retyping* what I'd already written. Granted, I could have done what some writers do—a lot of cutting and pasting—and I probably could have been more disciplined about what I put down on paper in the first place. But I tried to cut and paste and I tried to be more disciplined, and neither worked.

The benefits of word processing go beyond the time and drudgery you're spared and the magical things you can do when you're revising. Because a processor enables you to type much faster (and with much less effort) than even a good electric typewriter (there is no need on a processor to use carriage return), you're able to get your thoughts down more quickly, thus reducing the likelihood of forgetting what you want to say. What's more, simply *knowing* that revising is going to be relatively painless takes the heat off during the normally punishing first-draft stage of most writing projects. You don't fall into the trap, so common among even professional writers, of trying to produce too "finished" a manuscript too soon in the process.

The bottom line? As I suggested earlier, if you're able to produce a reasonably finished first draft (and by "reasonably finished," I'm talking about a draft you can edit or revise with pencil or pen), a processor is probably a luxury, even though it *will* save you additional typing time. On the other hand, if you're forever revising and forever putting sheets into the typewriter and then yanking them out three or four sentences later, the picture changes. You may have to do some calculations and figure out, as I did, how much of your writing time—and energy—is being spent simply reproducing what you've already produced. But if you find this number exceeds 25 percent, a visit to your local computer center might well be in order, even if you have to precede it with a visit to your local bank.

4 | Getting It Together

Most writing courses and "how-to" writing books give so little shrift to all but the pure *mechanics* of the process—how you choose words and hammer together sentences—you would almost think that everything else you need to do when you write, like gathering, pondering, and organizing your material, is superfluous to the whole business, not unlike the stretching exercises you're supposed to do—but often neglect to do—before you run or play tennis.

Would that it were true. The fact of the matter is that in many writing situations—and my point applies to professionals and nonprofessionals alike—the time and effort you devote to gathering and organizing your material has as much bearing on the quality of the finished product as whatever degree of verbal dexterity you bring to the process. What's more, the time and effort you devote to gathering and organizing almost always have a bearing on the amount of time and effort you have to expend when you finally get around to the actual writing.

I like to refer to these preliminary aspects of writing (i.e., anything you do in connection with the writing that doesn't involve actually putting words down on paper) as the "nonwording'' elements of the process, and I was interested to learn not long ago that the typical professional writer, according to one study, spends considerably more time (66 percent) on the non-wording aspects of writing than do novice writers (33 percent). Professional writers, in other words, recognize that to write effectively you need to be more than simply an accomplished wordsmith.

I myself was ignorant of this principle for many years and I paid a heavy price for my ignorance. Under the delusion that the fundamental challenge in writing was to conjure glitzy words and then weave these words into impeccably structured sentences, I wasn't always as organized as I should have been when I was doing what I considered the ''coolie'' work— researching my articles and books. And the less disciplined and systematic I was, the more time, effort, and irritation it invariably cost me. I can remember a number of occasions spending the better part of a morning simply trying to *find* my notes, and more often than I care to recall having to make long distance phone calls to people I'd *already* interviewed—not because I needed new information but because I couldn't for the life of me decipher my handwritten notes. I can also recall, without pleasure, a few occasions in which I started to write an article without having gathered *enough* information, which may not be exactly the same as squeezing blood from a stone but surely approximates the experience. And while I usually managed to grind out something publishable, these situations stick in my mind as some of the most painful writing episodes in my career.

That's why in this chapter I'd like to offer some specific ideas on two aspects of writing that most books on writing ignore but that most accomplished writers recognize as being crucial: how you record your research and what you do with the research once you've gathered it.

The Pleasures—and Hazards—of Researching

Gathering research these days is a good deal easier than it used to be before there were telephones, tape recorders, copy machines, and computer data bases. Ironically, though, the very ease with which it's possible to gather research today carries certain risks.

First of all, because you don't have to work as hard anymore to record research (it's a lot easier to photocopy a page than to take notes), there's a tendency to gather far more information than you really need or can organize efficiently; so, when the time comes to organize your material, you're so flooded with information you don't know where to begin.

Then, too, when you become too automated in your research techniques, you deny yourself the perspective that develops when you're forced to be more selective about what you gather and more painstaking in how you record it.

There are other hazards as well. Time, for example. Unless you're deep into tax-exempts or are working on a project for which you're being royally paid, you need to set limits on the amount of time you spend on research. And if you're working on a project that's of compelling interest to you, you need to be careful that you don't get so wrapped up in the research, you lose sight of the reason *behind* the research. It's been said that William Shirer, while researching *The Rise and Fall of the Third Reich,* didn't actually begin writing the book until the day the librarian barred him from the small room in which he had been gathering research for more than a year. "Go home, Mr. Shirer," the librarian is supposed to have told the author. "You have enough research to write five books."

The Art of Taking Notes

Being able to take notes efficiently is a more important skill for journalists and students than it is for businesspeople, but there are many situations in which even businesspeople have to gather information, either from source material or other people. For this reason, it's a topic that warrants discussion.

The key point here is that you not only gather *enough* of the information you need but that you record it in a way that won't create havoc for you when the time comes to write. Meeting this dual challenge is not usually a problem when you're gathering research from written sources—magazines, papers, books, etc.—but it gets a little trickier when you have to take notes while you're talking to someone in person or over the phone. On the one hand, you want to make sure you're taking down the information as comprehensively and as accurately as you can. But on the other hand, you can't allow *your* need to be accurate and comprehensive to inconvenience the people you're interviewing, especially in business situations.

With this problem in mind, it might be useful to review some of the methods used by accomplished professionals. Stanley Englebardt, a roving editor of the *Reader's Digest,* usually takes his interview notes on sheets of manila paper folded in fours, numbering each quadrant as he goes along and using his own system of shorthand in which he omits nearly all "vwls." Curry Kirkpatrick, a senior writer at *Sports Illustrated,* uses a three-by-five spiral pad that he can tuck into his pocket, but Ken Woodward, a *Newsweek* editor, is happiest when he has a large pad on a clipboard. "It's a question of psychic space," he explains. "When I have a big pad, I have plenty of room on the side to make little notes and I can then work on the notes when I'm coming back home on the train."

None of the professionals just mentioned, you may have noticed, uses a tape recorder, and they are not unusual in this respect. Reasons vary. Some professionals feel that a tape recorder inhibits the person being interviewed (a point I would argue since it's been my experience that once you get into a conversation that's being recorded, most people you're interviewing simply forget the tape recorder is even there). Others don't want to risk a malfunction during an interview or a tape breaking during transcription.

The main reason, however, most professional writers I know would rather take notes than use a tape recorder has to do with efficiency. Frank Deford, a senior writer at *Sports Illustrated* who does marvelous profiles, says that most of what gets recorded in an interview isn't of use anyway and so you end up wasting a lot of time going through your tapes. And Betsy Weinstock observes that when you use a tape recorder, nothing gets "weighted." She says she'd rather select the important quotes as she goes along.

Not that there aren't compelling advantages to using a tape recorder. A tape recorder, after all, captures *everything* that gets said in the interview, including nuances you could well miss if you were taking notes. A tape recorder frees you from at least some of the burden of taking notes (although it's always a good idea to take rough notes even while the recorder is on— just in case), and eliminates having to ask the person you're interviewing to slow down or repeat an answer because you haven't had time to record your notes. A tape recorder can also be valuable if you're working on a particularly sensitive subject. If you're ever challenged to document the note, you have it on tape.

My own criteria for using a tape recorder—and the criteria that most professional writers use—is keyed to the kind of project I'm working on and, in particular, to the length of the interview. I've found a tape recorder indispensable for all the as-told-to books I've ever worked on, and also for any articles in which I've had to interview the same person on several different occasions. I've found it less useful for articles in which

I've had to collect information from a number of different sources.

But tape recorder or no, there are two additional points about interviewing worth stressing here. The first has to do with a skill that Gay Talese, among others, considers the single most important element of interviewing: listening. Describing listening as a "discipline in and of itself," Talese insists that if you take the time to *develop* this discipline, you can learn to retain nearly everything you hear in an interview that might run as long as three hours—without taking notes and without, as he puts it, "slapping a machine down on the table."

The second point worth bearing in mind is that no matter what your system of taking notes is, try to get into the habit of reading over and, if need be, organizing those notes as *soon as possible* after the conversation. One travel writer I know— David Butwin—will take time at several intervals throughout the day to put his notes into a more finished form, and Frank Deford warns that if you don't organize your notes while they are still fresh in your mind, you'll probably forget things you would have otherwise remembered. "You sometimes think at the time," Deford says, "that you have such a good grasp of what you've heard that you'll be able to recall it later with a few key words. What you have to remember, though, is that a day or two later, what seemed so vivid at the time can be gone."

Taking Command of Your Information

No less important than the manner in which you *record* information is what you do with it once you've assembled it. The mistake many novice writers—students in particular— make repeatedly is to start writing too soon in the process, before they've taken sufficient command of their material. They don't allow enough time for the information they've gathered to settle and crystallize.

The aspect of writing I'm talking about here is usually referred to as "organization," and different writers describe the process in different ways. Martin Marty talks about the need to "internalize your material so that you are no longer a prisoner to your index cards." A. E. Hotchner sees it as a process of not only assimilating but of "filtering the material through the grist of your personality." Ken Woodward stresses the need to read and reread your notes not so much to "learn" the material but to "feel the story in your bones." And the late Jim Fixx likened this aspect of writing to "cramming for finals in college."

To appreciate how important this phase of writing is, you need only consider the lengths to which most professional writers go to organize, assimilate, and gain control of their material. At the very least, nearly all professional writers read over their research material not just once or twice but as many as a dozen times, and many writers have developed specific systems for assimilating and organizing.

Richard Chesnoff, a free-lancer who was once the executive editor of *Newsweek International,* goes through a step he calls "editing" his notes. He reads through his notebooks, checks important points with a magic marker, and then types the important points on a fresh sheet of paper. This typewritten sheet now becomes the foundation for his article.

Other writers have devised more elaborate classification systems.

Roger Williams, a former *Time* correspondent who now free-lances, takes voluminous notes in a stenographer's notebook (he'll fill as many as three notebooks for a typical three-thousand word article) and then puts together his own index, noting for each name and topic the notebook and the page. "It takes a lot of time," he admits. "But by the time I'm finished with the index, I feel as if I'm in control of my subject."

John Fuller divides the subject of the books he works on into categories and assigns to each category a file. Assuming he has, say, twelve categories, he then numbers each file from 100 to 1200 and numbers each note or clipping sequentially according to the folder it belongs to. Folder number 300, for instance, might be entitled "Congressional Hearings" and might include as many as forty separate pieces of information numbered 300 to 340. To keep track of each entry, he records all the entries from each folder into a spiral notebook. "I can run my finger down a page," he says, "and come up with the note I'm looking for.

A. E. Hotchner not only keeps his notes in folders but he has developed an intriguing method of *using* these notes when he's actually writing. He stretches a clothesline across his office and attaches each page of typewritten notes on the line with a clothespin or clip. On some days, he may have as many as two hundred notes pinned all over his office. "It looks chaotic," he says, "but it works well for me. I like having that information out there where I can get to it easily. It also gets me off my rear."

Sound compulsive? Small potatoes compared to Gay Talese. Talese, once he's typed his notes, organizes them into file folders that he keeps, not in *file cabinets,* but in shoe boxes. (The reason he prefers shoe boxes, he says, is that he can transport his files from Manhattan to his country place in New Jersey more easily than he could were his folders sitting in a file cabinet.) Talese has also set up an intricate filing system in which he custom-cuts his own index "tabs" out of three-by-five cards, uses a fine-tipped Japanese pen to write on each card a capsule summary of the material in each file folder, and then staples each tab to the folder in such a pattern that at a glance, he can gain a capsulized glimpse of the entire file. He then writes out a detailed reference card for each box.

Overkill? In many writing situations—especially routine memos, letters, and reports—yes. Talese, however, insists that given the prodigious research that goes into the kinds of books he writes, his ritualistic approach to organizing his material, with all of its administrative minutiae, serves a highly pragmatic function. "When you're writing anything in which you have to deal with a lot of different information," he says, "you have to become the master of your research. You need to be able to jump back and forth, and the only way you can do that is to make the material you gather *more* than just familiar to you. It has to become *part* of you."

5 | Figuring Out Where You Want to Go—and Getting There

Not long ago a sales executive at one of my seminars asked me to read over a letter he was writing to a customer he'd lost a few months before but was now trying to woo back. The letter, he explained was giving him "fits." He knew what he wanted to say but sensed, as he kept reading over what he'd written, that the letter wasn't working.

I took a look at the letter and recognized immediately why the salesman was having trouble. "Dear Mr. Zack," the letter began. "You claimed in a recent conversation that our company was giving you inadequate service. . . ."

You wouldn't think, would you, that you'd have to remind a successful sales executive that you don't woo ex-customers by starting a letter with, "You claimed in a recent conversation . . ." But the fact that it *was* necessary in this particular situation raises an important question. Why wasn't this sales executive able to recognize without my pointing it out that his opening sentence was likely to *alienate* his reader? Or, to expand the question, why is it so many people, as soon as they face the prospect of putting their thoughts down on paper, suddenly lose touch with so much of the knowledge, experience, and sensitivity they use routinely in other situations?

The obvious explanation for this paradox is not terribly complicated—not when you bear in mind everything the brain has to attend to during the act of writing itself. As I've already pointed out, the brain doesn't fare too well when it has to split its attention. So it's not hard to see how you can become so consumed by the trees you're hacking down when you write that you lose sight of the forest you're trying to clear.

This phenomenon—the fact that the very act of writing can blind you to what you already know—can be as much of a problem for professional writers as it is for nonprofessionals. It's not nearly as noticeable to the average reader. Before a piece of professional writing sees the light of print, remember, it is usually given the once over by professional editors whose specialty is finding—and, if need be, shoring up—any holes that may have eluded the notice of the writer. Most businesspeople and students who write don't have this cushion. And even when business correspondence or school papers do get scrutinized, the criticism is usually confined to style—the way the piece is *written*. And that's where the problem begins.

The point I'm driving at is well illustrated by the following letter, which is a composite, albeit exaggerated, of several letters I've collected from student writers.

March 11, 1985

Mr. D. Edward Beat
Deadbeat Associates
14 Dun Street
Philadelphia, Pa.

Dear Mr. Beat:

Benjamin Franklin once noted that creditors have better memories than debtors. So it's possible that the only reason I find it necessary to write you this letter is nothing more complicated than the fact that you have forgotten about the $580 you have owed us for the past ten months.

I recognize, of course, that in these busy and competitive times, it's easy to get bogged down in the daily pressures of business, and I'm sure that herein lies the explanation for why you have not answered any of the many phone calls we have made to your office over the past year or so, or have not responded to the monthly statements and reminders we have been sending you over the past several months.

I know, Mr. Beat, that as a businessperson you want to follow an honorable course. This is why I do not put much store in the statement attributed to you by your bookkeeper to the effect that you would pay us "when hell freezes over."

I am asking you, therefore, as one businessperson to another, to give this matter your personal attention as soon as you find it convenient to do so. I'm sure that you are as anxious to resolve this matter as we are.

If you have any questions, please feel free to contact me.

Sincerely yours,

E. Z. Goesit

There is nothing wrong with the way this letter is *written*. It is easy to understand, it has a nice tone, it flows well. If you were grading it in a business-writing course, you would give it at least a B.

The question, though, is whether the letter is likely to do the job for which it was obviously intended. Is it likely to produce a check? I doubt it.

Consider this revision:

March 11, 1985

Mr. D. Edward Beat
Deadbeat Associates
14 Dun Street
Philadelphia, Pa.

Dear Mr. Beat:

This morning, I sent your file to our lawyers, B. Breaker & Associates, with instructions to initiate legal action against you.

If you would like to prevent such action, have a certified check for $580 on my desk no later than April 3.

Sincerely,

Cary Bigstick

   The revision is much briefer than the original (and presumably would take a lot less time to write), but it clearly packs more muscle—not because of the way it's *written* but because of the thinking (and the threat) behind the message.

   Let's consider another example, this time from a letter I received not long ago from my local Salvation Army chapter. "Dear Friend," the letter began. "There has been a recent change in the territorial responsibility of the Norwalk post of The Salvation Army."

   Here again, we have information clearly conveyed, but I question whether the information is serving a productive purpose. The Salvation Army wants money from me and so it's obviously important that they capture my interest early in the letter. "Territorial responsibility" doesn't interest me. Nor is it likely to interest most people.

   What *would* interest me enough to read on? I can't say for sure. Maybe a provocative set of statistics. Maybe a brief anecdote about people in my community who are being helped by the Salvation Army. Whatever it is, it won't be the *writing* that interests me, it will be the thought behind the writing.

   Let's look at one more example that illustrates the same point, this one a letter from an insurance company pitching me on the idea of buying life insurance for my daughter.

Dear Parent:

We believe it is important to make available a complete insurance program to College and University students. It is important that life insurance be a part of this complete insurance program because it provides protection now and guarantees insurability in the future. For only $1, you can apply for this excellent $10,000 life insurance plan designed specifically to meet the unusual needs of active college students.

All the provisions of this policy remain in full effect 365 days a year (anywhere in the world) regardless of whether or not your child:
1. Enters the military
2. Flies a plane or sky-dives
3. Drives a motorcycle
4. Scuba dives
5. Leaves school.

In fact, the *only* restriction is the two-year suicide clause.

I read no further.

Forget for the moment the ineffective beginning of this letter (one of the worst mistakes you can make in a pitch letter is to tell the reader what you "believe" in). Instead, let's dwell briefly (very briefly) on the italics that drew my attention to the two-year suicide clause. I'm not sure how receptive I might have been, in general, to a pitch about life insurance for my daughter, but I know one thing for certain: I don't want to think about two-year suicide clauses.

Becoming a More "Strategic" Writer

Each of the examples you've just read illustrates what can happen when you worry too much about how something is *written* and not enough about what the writing does or doesn't accomplish. This is not to say, of course, that how clearly and concisely something is written is an issue that shouldn't occupy your attention. But as we've just seen, what if those thoughts—regardless of how clearly or concisely you've expressed them—aren't strategically keyed to the objective behind the thoughts. What if the thoughts, independent of how they're expressed, don't work? What if I, as a reader, have so little interest in the subject you're writing about that after I read the first sentence I deposit your letter in the nearest wastebasket? Or what if a fact you mention or some point you raise strikes so raw a nerve that I reject your entire message?

I know what some of you are thinking. Aren't the issues I'm

raising here related less to writing and more to thinking, to individual sensitivity, and to problem-solving? And couldn't you
argue that the ability to come up with the thoughts needed to
solve a problem is *independent* of the skill it takes to express that
solution in writing in a clear, concise manner?

You could indeed. You could also argue that in any number of
writing situations, your task is simply to communicate information, and you don't need to worry about arousing reader interest or avoiding sensitive areas. And you could argue, finally,
that even if these considerations did in fact embody *writing*
skills, how would you go about *teaching* people these skills?
Aren't we dealing here with a thinking process reflective of an
individual's intelligence, sensitivity, and experience?

I can't quarrel with any of these arguments, but I would like
to offer the following observations:

First, thinking up a solution to a problem and expressing that
solution in writing are indeed different mental functions. But
except for personal letters and assignments written for school,
you can't really separate the thoughts that are the essence of a
solution from the way you express those thoughts. Once you
leave school, you rarely write simply to "write"; you write because the writing has to accomplish an objective.

Second, there are indeed writing situations in which you
don't need to concern yourself with arousing the reader's interest, striking the appropriate tone, or eliciting a specific response, but these situations—in business, at least—are rare.

Third, the ability to come up with specific ideas to solve specific problems is, yes, a product of intelligence and experience.
But I contend that most people, when they write, are unable to
call upon much of the intelligence and experience they already
have, and I also contend that it's possible to mentally program
yourself to prevent this from happening.

Let us now look at two techniques that illustrate this possibility. One of them is something I call the Target Statement. The
other is something I call the Envisioning Chart.

The Target Statement

The Target Statement is nothing more than a statement of purpose meant to be written out *before* you begin to write. A simple enough technique on the surface, it could turn out to be the most valuable technique you learn in this book.

Consider for a moment what would have happened if the imaginary writer of the first of the letters you've just read—the letter to D. Edward Beat—had written down, "I want D. Edward Beat to send me the money he owes me *immediately.*" Would he have taken the *time* and *effort,* I wonder, to write so carefully worded a letter? Probably not. He would have recognized that the time for a tactful approach had long since passed.

A Target Statement is *not,* let me emphasize, a summary statement of what your memo or letter or report is about; it is, to repeat, a statement of your *objective*—of what you want to make happen (or to prevent from happening) with what you're writing. The reason you're writing a letter to a prospective employer, for instance, isn't merely to tell the prospective employer about yourself. You're writing to persuade the prospective employer to give you an interview. The reason you're writing an angry letter to the phone company is not simply cathartic—to tell the company how angry you are or how incompetent you think the phone company is; it's to get your phone service improved. If you're an advertising salesman writing to a client who is angry about a mix-up in schedules, your primary objective isn't to clarify the mix-up, it is to *pacify* the angry client.

The distinction I'm drawing here may seem inconsequential, but it's crucial. Time and again, what strikes me about the writing samples I critique in my corporate seminars is how difficult it is to figure out the basic point or direction of the correspondence. And time and again when I question the managers who've submitted these samples, I find that they themselves are not sure, either: they simply haven't given it much thought.

Even more important, though, when you don't take the time

to figure out, *before* you do anything else, what you're trying to accomplish, you have no yardstick by which to measure your progress, and you frequently fall into the trap of shuffling words around in the vague hope that somehow the words will simply "come together" and solve whatever problem you're trying to solve.

I'm not denying that by shuffling words around you can't end up once in a while with a piece of writing that works. And I'll grant, too, that sometimes it isn't *until* you've begun to shuffle words on paper that you begin to get a true fix on your target. Generally, though, when you begin putting your thoughts down on paper *before* you've decided what those thoughts are supposed to accomplish, you're inviting trouble and probably creating extra work for yourself. Yes, you may eventually end up where you want to be, but it will almost certainly take you longer to get there, and the ride en route is likely to be bumpy.

The Envisioning Chart

Knowing where you want to go is one thing. Figuring out the best way to get there is something else again. And figuring out a way to *teach* people how to figure out the best way to get where they want to go has been one of the most nettlesome challenges I've faced in my teaching.

Many people who teach writing (or write about writing) simply ignore the issue, assuming, I would imagine, that teaching people how to sell insurance, raise money, or talk their way through problem situations is better left to management consultants and sensitivity trainers. Those teachers who do tackle the issue usually stress the importance of analyzing your audience.

I've experimented with a number of different approaches designed to help people write more strategically but most of the suggestions I've come up with have fallen short and for the same reason: the specific strategies you adopt must invariably be determined by the situation that has prompted you to write in the first place. The trick, then, is to come up with an approach flexible enough to cover all writing situations but specific enough to provide a mental framework useful in individual situations.

I've come up with such an approach. I call it the Envisioning Chart, and it's based on the following idea: that apart from the information being conveyed in any written document and regardless of the style in which it's written, you can measure its success on the basis of a simple measure—whether or not it has had the desired impact on the person or people reading it. With this rationale in mind, I've identified four criteria that have to be met if this impact is to be achieved:

1. Reader interest
2. Reader understanding
3. Reader acceptance
4. Reader motivation

Let's examine briefly what I mean by each.

Reader interest.

Reader interest refers to how likely—or unlikely—your reader is to grant you the time needed to read whatever you've written. How interested your reader is in what you've written will vary, of course, not only according to the subject, but according to your relationship with the reader. (I don't care *what* they're writing about, I'm always interested in letters from my children.) As a general rule, though, it's risky to take reader interest for granted. I'm all but convinced that it's the failure of most people to concern themselves with attracting the interest of their readers that explains why the vast majority of what gets written today—particularly in business and government—never gets *read*.

Reader understanding.

Reader understanding refers, simply, to whether your readers are familiar enough with your information to understand what you're trying to tell them and is a particularly important criterion if you're a scientist or technician who writes to a nontechnical audience. Here, again, a gentle warning:

don't be too quick to *assume* that the people you write to are going to know what you're talking about, and don't worry as much as you may now be worrying about repeating things for fear of "insulting" your reader's intelligence. Think about it for a moment. How many times when *you've* been reading something have you ever been angry or felt insulted because the writer has taken special pains to make sure you understand a particular point?

Reader acceptance.

Reader acceptance is a more elusive criterion to define than interest and understanding. It has to do, generally speaking, with how your reader responds emotionally to you and to your material: whether or not you've been able—when the situation demands it—to gain your reader's empathy, trust, or confidence. The *tone* you strike—whether it's warm or cold, personal or impersonal—is certainly one factor in acceptance, but it's not the only factor. You also have to be careful (as we saw in the insurance letter above) that you don't raise issues that might alienate your reader. Even something as pedestrian as how your document looks—or the number of spelling errors in it—can affect acceptance.

Reader motivation.

Reader motivation has to do with whether or not you've given your reader a compelling enough reason to do whatever it is you want the reader to do. It isn't something you need to think about *every time* you write, but it's vital any time your aim is to produce a specific action.

Before I go any further, let me make two points about the four criteria I've just described.

To begin with, each of the four criteria is affected to one degree or another by how you actually express your thoughts on paper, but it's essential to recognize that these criteria transcend style. All things being equal, you can be deficient stylistically but still succeed in your writing if you manage to meet these criteria. By contrast, it doesn't matter how stylistically accomplished you are: if you don't meet the criteria, your effort will be wasted.

Second, the importance of each criterion to the success of the transaction will vary according to each individual writing situation. Sometimes you'll have to figure out a way to attract interest; other times you can take it for granted. Sometimes you'll have to be extremely careful about tone and about the information you deliver; other times it won't matter what you say or how you say it: the reader will accept it.

What's important, though, is that you take *all* of these criteria into account not *while* you're writing, but *before* you begin to write. Only then will you create the mental framework necessary to order your thinking strategically.

That's why it's well worth your time to begin each writing task by asking yourself a series of questions that make up the Envisioning Chart.

The Questions	Contingency Actions
Do I know what I want to accomplish?	
Yes	
Not necessarily ⟶	Ask yourself what you you'd like to see happen— or not happen— as the result of what you've written.
Can I accomplish this objective with what I'm writing?	

Yes
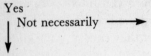
| Not necessarily ——————▶   Figure out another approach.
▼

Do I have enough
information to
accomplish my objective?

Yes
| Not necessarily ——————▶   Gather the information you
▼   need.

Are my readers likely
to be interested enough
in the information
I'm delivering to begin
reading and to stay with
me?

Yes
| Not necessarily ——————▶   Put yourself in your reader's
▼   place and complete the following
                                       statement: "This is important
                                       to me because . . ."

Will my audience
understand with-
out any difficulty
the points I want to
get across?

Yes
| Not necessarily ——————▶   Try to relate unfamiliar
▼   points to the reader's
                                       own experience.

Are there sensitive areas
I have to be aware
of that could influence
my reader to reject my
ideas?

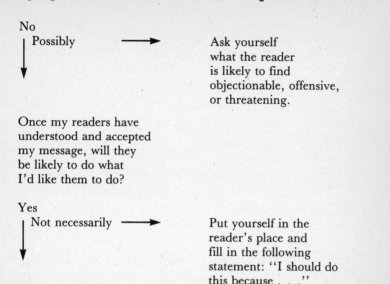

No
| Possibly   ⟶   Ask yourself
↓   what the reader
                                     is likely to find
                                     objectionable, offensive,
                                     or threatening.

Once my readers have
understood and accepted
my message, will they
be likely to do what
I'd like them to do?

Yes
| Not necessarily   ⟶   Put yourself in the
↓   reader's place and
                                     fill in the following
                                     statement: "I should do
                                     this because . . ."

This chart is not an "outline," although it could certainly be used as a basis of an outline. Let me also emphasize that the questions may be ones you are already asking yourself intuitively as you write. In any event, it shouldn't take you more than a couple of minutes to walk yourself through the chart. And considering what those two minutes will do to focus your attention on what you need to do to accomplish your writing objective, they could be the most important two minutes you spend throughout the entire writing episode.

The Satellite Outline

Just everybody agrees that it's a swell idea to outline your thoughts before you get too involved in the verbal carpentry that goes into the actual writing. The only trouble with this swell idea is that maybe one person out of a hundred has the kind of well-ordered mind you need in order to put together a logically organized outline early on in the writing task. I, for one, have always had difficulties with outlines, and in high school, whenever we were instructed to submit an outline with our papers, I would generally write the outline *after* I'd written the paper.

All of which underscores the usefulness of a technique I call the Satellite Outline. Pictured on page 65, the Satellite Outline may look at first like nothing more than a jazzier alternative to the conventional outline, but there is more here than meets the eye.

First of all, the Satellite Outline is easier to work with than the standard linear outline: you don't run into the logistical problem of where to stick point D under Roman numeral II once you've already started listing points under Roman numeral III. Each time you come up with an idea, you simply connect it, via a line and a circle enclosing the thought, to whatever circle it attaches to. You almost never run out of room.

With this added ease comes more flexibility. No longer obliged to formulate ideas according to a specific sequence, you're able to think more freely, and your ideas, as they emerge and take shape on the outline, assume a logic more or less naturally. Finally, the *visual* aspect of the Satellite Outline is itself a clarifying agent: working with circles instead of lists gives you a clearer perspective of your overall presentation and makes it easier to set priorities and to see how everything connects.

As the illustrations on the following page indicate, the Satellite Outline can be used in different ways. The first Satellite Outline depicted represents a general outline for this chapter. The Satellite Outline that follows covers the information in the preceding two paragraphs and illustrates how the same technique might be used for an individual section in a chapter. It doesn't matter how detailed or how general you want to make the outline: the technique will work either way. I use the Satellite Outline for full-length articles (usually making adjustments as I go along), and, when I'm not sure of how my thoughts ought to come together, I'll use it for individual paragraphs. I know executives who use the technique for all of their memos and, in particular, for dictation. All told, in fact, I would say that the Satellite Outline is the one technique that the majority of my students have found the more useful than any other.

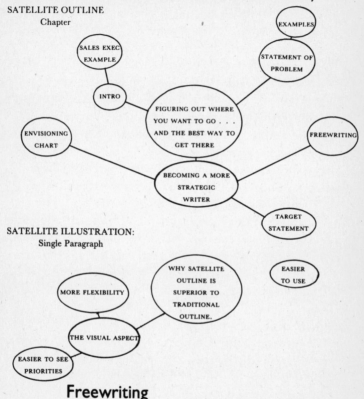

SATELLITE OUTLINE
Chapter

EXAMPLES

SALES EXEC EXAMPLE

STATEMENT OF PROBLEM

INTRO

FIGURING OUT WHERE YOU WANT TO GO . . . AND THE BEST WAY TO GET THERE

ENVISIONING CHART

FREEWRITING

BECOMING A MORE STRATEGIC WRITER

TARGET STATEMENT

SATELLITE ILLUSTRATION:
Single Paragraph

WHY SATELLITE OUTLINE IS SUPERIOR TO TRADITIONAL OUTLINE.

EASIER TO USE

MORE FLEXIBILITY

THE VISUAL ASPECT

EASIER TO SEE PRIORITIES

Freewriting

Freewriting is a technique closely associated with writer and teacher Peter Elbow and is based on the generally accepted notion that apart from its other pressures, writing calls for two mental activities that are not only different but not particularly compatible: the first is generating thoughts; the second is criticizing the thoughts and how you've expressed them. Both of these mental activities are obviously essential to writing. You need to generate ideas when you write and you need to view these ideas critically—to see if they fit into your overall conceptual scheme and to make sure you've expressed them clearly and concisely. The problem, though, is what happens when you try to *combine* these functions—that is, when you try to generate and criticize thoughts at the same time. One side of your brain wants to get somewhere as quickly as possible. The other side wants to fuss over each step.

Freewriting eases the internal tug of war. What you do when you freewrite is allow the creative or generative side of your mind to operate—for a while at least—unfettered by the judgments of your more critical side. You simply let yourself disgorge thoughts as fast as you can write them down. You don't worry about choosing the "right" word (you put, say, "blah blah" when you can't think of the precise word). You don't worry about spelling (you can use your own shorthand system). You don't worry about punctuation or sentence structure or anything *mechanical*. You simply try to get as many thoughts down on paper as you can without—and this is important—*judging* whether the thoughts are correct, articulate, or even on target. If you can't think of something to write, you write whatever pops into your mind, regardless of how silly or irrelevant it might seem.

I'd never heard of freewriting until I read Elbow's book *Writing with Power* (Oxford University Press, New York, 1981) but I have since found the technique an enormous help in my day-to-day writing. I used to be one of those writers in whom the impulse to criticize was so strong that I would not allow myself to move from one sentence to the next until I was convinced that I had achieved "perfection." Little wonder that my writing was so labored. Little wonder I was lucky on some days to turn out a single page of finished manuscript!

Freewriting has freed me from this compulsion and has improved both the quantity and, I think, the quality of my writing. Yes, I still fuss over my sentences and I'm still superjudgmental, but I have disciplined myself—and it wasn't easy, by any means—to *suspend* judgment until *after* I've had a chance to air my thoughts on paper.

Freewriting works best, I think, as a preliminary to what you would normally consider your first draft. You do it after you've assembled and assimilated your notes, written out a target statement, gone through the Envisioning chart, and completed a Satellite Outline. What I generally do when I'm working on a first draft is to freewrite for maybe three or four minutes. I *then* go back and do some rough revising. My goal, in any case, is to get *something* down on paper in the way of a first draft before I start fretting about whether the words are precise enough and the sentences read smoothly enough.

What's noteworthy about freewriting is that nearly all the writers I know who write with relative ease *use* the freewriting technique, or some version of it. Marilyn Machlowitz always begins a writing project with what she calls a "zero draft," her only objective in this draft to fill the paper with thoughts. And A. E. Hotchner has devised his own shorthand system for first drafts so that when he does his first draft, his pencil can keep up with his thoughts.

When I work with freewriting in my seminars, I have participants write the same document, whether it be a letter or a memo, two different ways. First, they spend about five minutes working on it the way they would normally write. A half-hour or so later, I ask them to freewrite the document for about three minutes. I then have them compare the versions.

The exercise is somewhat manipulative; by the time the students do the freewriting version, they've had some time to think about the piece. But even with this qualification, the results are still revealing.

To begin with, nearly everybody is able to produce *more* writing in less time when they freewrite. So, if nothing else—regardless of how incoherent the freewriting version may be—it's safe to say that when you freewrite you generate more material.

I then have students compare the number of thoughts in each version. Here, again, most people report more thoughts in the freewriting version and here, again, no surprise. When you're not picking apart each thought as it emerges, you get more of them on paper.

What's really interesting, though, is what happens when I ask people to read over the freewritten version and give their reaction to it. In about half the instances, students are surprised at how "good" it sounds. "It flows better," people will say. "It's more like me—the way I talk," another person will say.

Usually, of course, most people tell me that they'd have to make any number of changes in the freewritten version: tighten it, soften it, make it a little less casual. But nearly everybody agrees that *once* they've freewritten, they're in a much better position to make the necessary changes. Not long ago a student observed that freewriting enabled him to "get out in the open" what he really wanted to say in what turned out to be a politically sensitive memo. "Getting my own feelings out of the way," he observed, "helped me see more clearly what I had to do about the problem."

Freewriting, I should caution, takes practice. Your judgmental side (your "left" brain) doesn't like to relinquish control. (That's the point of writing *fast:* not to leave time for judgments. Novelist Leonard Michaels says he is so judgmental he can't write page two until he's satisfied with page one. "So I rewrite page one twenty-five times," he says, "then page two, and meanwhile I'm dying to get to page thirty.") So be warned. The best way to incorporate freewriting into your writing routine is in increments. Start with one minute of freewriting. Then expand it thirty seconds at a time. See if you can extend the amount of time you spend freewriting to at least ten minutes. But whatever you do, try it. As Elbow explains, "Probably the major benefit of freewriting is that it will solve what for many people is the biggest problem in writing— getting started. Since you set no expectations when you freewrite, other than to fill a page with material, you have no pressure on you and you work as fast as you can, without worry."

6 Patterns: The Key to Fluid Writing

Nearly everything we've covered so far has involved aspects of writing over which you can assume at least a small measure of conscious control. Adopting a more positive mental attitude, creating a more efficient writing environment, being more systematic in your research and organizing methods, taking the time beforehand to think out an overall writing strategy—there is nothing mystical about any of these steps. Incorporating them into your writing is mainly a matter of deciding you want to do it, and doing it.

In this chapter, however, we will be dealing with the writing episode itself—the actual business of stitching together sentences and building paragraphs, and here, I'm afraid, the ground rules change. For once we leave the nonwording elements of writing and plunge into the writing itself, it becomes all but impossible to actively *control* the process.

Yes, you can orient your thinking in a general direction and you can think to yourself, "Now what do I want to *say?*" And after something appears on paper, you can ask yourself, "How does that *sound?*"

But, as Frank Smith points out in *Writing and the Writer,*

(Holt, Rinehart & Winston, 1982), you don't really *choose* words as you're writing—not in the normal, purposeful sense of the word. The words simply *occur*, as a natural representation of the thoughts you're trying to express.

Given this fact—that strictly speaking much of what determines the outcome of the writing episode is not really a matter of conscious choice—it is logical to ask how writing happens and why certain people have more ability than others to write clearly, concisely, and smoothly.

I don't pretend to have the ultimate answer to these questions, but I have a thought or two that relate in no small way to the theme of this book.

I now believe that the ability to express ideas effectively on paper is rooted in what might best be described as certain patterns of expression—patterns that have been already programmed into your brain *before* you sit down to write.

The patterns I'm referring to here, it's important to stress, are independent of the particular subject you're writing about, independent of the information you are trying to convey, and independent, too, of whatever intelligence may lie behind the information. The patterns simply represent the *form* in which the information arrives on paper.

To illustrate what I mean by a "pattern," consider a sentence that recently appeared in a John Leonard television review written for *New York* magazine. Describing the title character of a new television series about a police psychiatrist, Leonard wrote: "She is also a Mary Lou Retton at prognosis; she always scores tens."

A nice way of making a point, yes? But nothing mysterious here. Embodied in this sentence are three different techniques: an analogy (likening the title character's prognosis ability to the gymnastic skill of an Olympic champion); the use of a familiar public figure in that analogy (Mary Lou Retton); and the juxtaposition of a general statement ("the Mary Lou Retton of prognosis") and a specific explanation of that statement ("She always scores tens").

I call this a "pattern" because it could work in any number

of situations. If I were writing about a politician, for instance, I might put together the following sentence: "He is the Reggie Jackson of politics: he gets his biggest hits when everybody's watching." And if I were describing a businesswoman, I might write: "She is the Howard Cosell of big business: everybody complains about her, but everybody listens when she talks." Different words, different people, but the same pattern.

As you can see, the patterns I'm referring to are not related so much to the specific *words* that ultimately express specific thoughts, but to the manner in which the ideas behind the words are packaged to produce a particular effect in a given situation: whether it's to communicate a message as simply and as succinctly as possible, deliver a persuasive argument, or, as in the Leonard example, make a wry observation. The patterns, in other words, produce thoughts in a way that meets certain reader-oriented requirements.

Let me dwell for a moment on this distinction, not only because it seems to me so crucial but because it's a distinction that most people fail to draw. As I've been stressing throughout this book, the chief reason so many people have so much difficulty writing is that they approach writing as essentially a wording enterprise and consequently do not address the broader issues of objectives and strategy. Similarly, most people pay little attention when they write to the patterns I'm talking about, and to how these patterns contribute to or impede the readability of a written presentation. Many people, in other words, are able to *express* their ideas on paper well enough, but because the ideas have not been packaged in readable patterns, the ideas don't *read* well. In particular, many people fail to appreciate the difficulties inherent in reading and fail to see that if readers are to grasp the meaning of the thoughts being conveyed, the sentences that deliver these thoughts must be structured and ordered according to criteria that vary little from reading situation to reading situation.

Skilled writers are different. Skilled writers, intuitively or consciously, express their ideas in patterns keyed to the demands of the reading experience. Skilled writers possess what might best be described as an "ear" for the particular kind of writing in which they specialize—an ability to sense how well something is going to work once it's down on paper. So, even when the writing misses the mark, as it often does in early drafts, skilled writers usually know how to *revise:* they can do some chipping here and some sanding there and wind up with a finished product that has about it the obvious aura of craftsmanship.

Let us not worry for now about whether the patterns I'm talking about here are an outgrowth of a broader range of intellectual skills or if you simply *develop* these patterns through extensive reading or through writing itself. The point is that whether you're writing a novel, a poem, or an article, you don't consciously *select* these patterns *as* you're writing (not the first time around, anyway), in the deliberate, purposeful way that a carpenter selects a specifically-sized drill bit. The decision-making process occurs far too quickly and involves far too many cognitive decisions to allow for deliberation. It would be more accurate to compare the "decisions" of skilled writers with the "moves" of a skilled basketball player or a jazz pianist: instinctive and always in response to a given set of circumstances.

Developing an "Instrument"

If writing ability, as I've proposed, is rooted in the presence of certain patterns of expression, the question is how you build these patterns into the "instrument" you use when you write. How do you program yourself, in other words, to write more effectively?

I ran into this problem as soon as I began teaching. Time and again, in reading over student papers, I was able to revise paragraphs that had been clumsily written. But other than the fact that the changes felt right to *me,* I was rarely able to communicate the rationale behind the revision.

Here's an example of what I'm talking about.

The student board of directors is the supervisory body within the Teen Center facility. Their decisions are final. The student board elects two or three students from each high school level. All attempts are made to have equal representation of all high schools. Within the Teen Center facility, the student board makes decisions about programs and activities, and approves with the director staff positions. The student board is also the first group to deal with any disciplinary actions. The director of the F.T.C. is a nonvoting member of the student board.

There is nothing complicated about the ideas the writer is trying to convey. The paragraph is grammatically sound and written in a simple, straightforward style. Still, it is not an easy paragraph to *read*. The ideas don't track well; they jump around, and you have trouble following the jumps. What's wrong here, in short, is that there's an incompatability between the way the ideas are presented and the way we need to receive these ideas as readers if we are to make sense of them.

Consider this revision:

The Teen Center is supervised by a board of directors made up entirely of students who represent local high schools. The students make all key decisions. They decide the programs and activities the Teen Center should run, and they approve all the staff appointments made by the director. They are also the first group to deal with any disciplinary actions. Included on the board is the Teen Center director, but he doesn't have a vote.

The obvious difference between these two paragraphs is that the second is much easier to read and understand. The less obvious difference between the two is that the ideas in the second are packaged in patterns that *make* it more readable.

I've spent a long time trying to isolate these patterns. What I did mostly was read over and over passages from accomplished writers like John McPhee, Gay Talese, John Gregory Dunne, Nora Ephron, Joan Didion, and Paul Theroux, not to familiarize myself with the words they chose but to see if I could identify the patterns that were common to all of the writers.

I found many such patterns. I found, for instance, that all of these writers usually make it a practice of placing the subject and the verb of each sentence at or near the beginning of the sentence and almost always together. I found that all of these writers seem to take special pains, either by repeating certain words or by using certain phrases, to tie one sentence to another sentence. What I found, all told, is that for every effect a writer is able to achieve—clarity, emphasis, cohesion—there is invariably a pattern that can explain the effect—a pattern, moreover, that is transferable to other writing situations. My guess was that if I could get my students to consciously recognize and then incorporate into their own writing repertoire similar patterns, they, too, would be able to produce writing that reads clearly, concisely, and smoothly (assuming, of course—and this is no small assumption—that they were able to come up with and organize ideas that were *worth* expressing).

I didn't invent these patterns—or the techniques that underlie them. There are, however, a number of patterns that seem to me to be basic to all writing transactions. These are the patterns that assure clarity, cohesion, and flow—qualities as important to business and technical reports as they are to articles and full-length books. These are patterns I'll be talking about in the next three chapters.

But before I get to these patterns, let me stress one final point—the fact that effective writing is itself a *pattern*. So even though I'll be talking about individual patterns in the next two chapters, keep in mind that it's the ability to use several patterns at once that will determine, in the end, how effectively—and painlessly—you write. In this respect at least, learning how to write with less pain is not unlike learning how to hit a tennis ball, shoot a basketball, or execute a difficult gymnastics stunt: you can isolate specific elements of the movement (i.e., bend your knees or shift your weight in a certain way, etc.) but until you can execute everything together without having to *think* about it, you won't be notably successful at any of these things.

So, as you read about each of these patterns, remember that the goal here goes beyond merely understanding the patterns and being able to consciously put into practice the techniques that underlie the patterns. Your goal, ultimately, is to incorporate these patterns into your overall mental approach so that you can use them without having to consciously think about the technique. It will take time, and, at first, when you're unfamiliar with a technique, it could slow down your writing. Stay with it. The more you *use* the techniques as you write, the more comfortable you'll become with them and the sooner you'll be able to forget about the techniques and let the patterns take care of themselves.

The *OR* in ORSON stands for Orienting, and represents what you did in the example above when you introduced your-self and explained why you were calling. The idea behind Orienting is that before people are ready to *listen* to you (or read what you've written), they need to be oriented: they need to know who you are and what you want.

The *SO* part of ORSON represents Spelling Out: delivering the particulars of your message. The *N* stands for Nailing Down, which is what you did when you asked for the contribu-tion.

Let's look now at how ORSON works in written communi-cation. Below are two letters, consisting of identical informa-tion. The only difference between the two is that the second follows the ORSON model and the first does not. Read each and then decide for yourself which flows more logically.

April 11, 1985

To: Parents of Prospective Diploma Mill U. Summer Program Stu-dents

Dear Parent:

Diploma Mill University is having an open house on Saturday morn-ing, April 28, in the Fast Buck Armory, on the campus of Diploma Mill University.

The Open House will start at 11 A.M. and run until 1 P.M. We'll be serving coffee and refreshments.

The Open House is for all prospective Diploma Mill parents and stu-dents.

Chances are, we have had an opportunity to talk with your son or daughter about the Pre-University Summer Program, which is now in its fourth year.

I have enclosed a map that tells you how to get to the Fast Buck Ar-mory. But if you have any additional questions or concerns, please contact me at my office (245-6200) or at my home after 7 P.M. (752-9099).

The Open House will start at 11 A.M. and run until 1 P.M. We'll be serving coffee and refreshments.

I have enclosed a map that tells you how to get to the Fast Buck Armory. But if you have any additional questions or concerns, please contact me at my office (245-6200) or at my home after 7 P.M. (752-9099).

Sincerely,

Jennifer Blake

Putting ORSON to Work

ORSON is fairly easy to use and works particularly well in business correspondence. Let's review its basic components:

- *OR: Orienting.* Orienting involves two kinds of information: first, whatever background informatin your readers need to know in order to understand *why* they should read your document; second—and perhaps more important—information that indicates the *particular direction or the purpose of your document.*
- *SO: Spelling Out.* The Spelling-Out component of your document consists of the specific information that relates to your objective. The length of this section will depend entirely on how much information you have to convey.
- *N: Nailing Down.* Nailing Down is leaving your reader with a definite idea of where you stand or what you would like to see happen *next.* In general, the Nailing Down part of the memo shouldn't run longer than a sentence or two.

Now that you understand the general concept of the model, let's look at some specific examples, first a memo, then a letter.

Date: April 25, 1789
To: William Bligh
From: Fletcher Christian
Subject: Public Floggings

Bill,

As you probably know, there has been a great deal of flak in the company about our new policy of subjecting to a public flogging any employee who is late more than twice in any one month. There has been so much grumbling, in fact, that we're falling behind in our production schedule.

I know how important you consider punctuality—and I agree with you. And you know, too, that I have always supported your policies in the past. This time, however, I question whether the policy is serving the company's best interests.

In the first place, have you any idea of how expensive it is these days to hire a professional flogger? The going rate for hackers is $400 an hour. And if you want somebody who really looks the part—the hood and everything—you have to figure $600 an hour, plus travel expenses.

Secondly, we don't have a suitable place to hold the floggings. The cafeteria people are getting a lot of complaints from maintenance about having to rearrange the chairs all the time.

Finally, it's questionable if the policy is really working. Of the 21 employees who've been flogged, 20 have quit. (The other one asked for an additional flogging.)

I suggest we get together soon to come up with an alternative policy. I know where we can pick up a good stretch rack very inexpensively.

Fletcher

II, LX B. C.

Emperor Claudius Caesar Nero
The Royal Palace
Rome

Dear Emperor Nero:

I was at the Baths last night with Helius, who suggested that I write you about a new catering service we've introduced at our restaurant, The IV Seasons—a service that could add an exciting new dimension to your orgies.

We now put together what I do not hesitate to call the best antipasto tray this side of Gaul. And, thanks to our new chariot service, we can deliver it to you within III hours after you place your order.

What I'd like to emphasize about this tray is that it contains a truly varied selection of food—enough of a selection to satiate *all* of your guests. The special antipasto tray combines, among other things, anchovies, sausage, green peppers, tomatoes, prosciutto and melon—plus an intriguing new food we now import from Palestine called chopped liver.

With your permission, I'd love to give you, free of charge, one of the trays so that you can see—and taste—for yourself what we offer. Give me the word, and I'll send over my chariot driver—I think he used to work for you: his name is Ben—with the tray.

By the way, how are the violin lessons coming?

Phillipus Sardini

The Importance of Orienting

The examples you've just read illustrate the versatility of ORSON and should give you an idea of how to use the technique in your own memos and letters. To use ORSON effectively, however, you must master I consider the most important component of the model—the Orienting. Why is it so important? Because if you don't orient properly, you could lose your reader before he's finished with the first paragraph.

If orienting is to be successful, it must do two things: first, it must establish a *positive* connection with your reader; second, it must tell the reader where you intend to go in your letter or memo.

In general, there are three ways you can accomplish these two objectives:

1. *Give background information.*

A short sentence or two that gives background information is the most widely used and simplest orienting device in business. I recommend giving this background information even if the "subject" line of the memo indicates the reason for writing. Remember, the person reading the memo might be receiving several different memos from different people about the same subject. The background information serves as a "reminder" of what aspect of the subject *your* message will cover. For example:

As you are aware, Employee Relations has been conducting a nonexempt compensations study in conjunction with Human Resources. There is finally an end in sight, and I would like you to know what the time schedule will be.

As you know, we've been getting a lot of complaints of late about slow deliveries. I've looked into the matter and have come up with a few recommendations.

2. *Make a personal connection.*

Making a personal connection means establishing some link between you and the person to whom you're writing and is an excellent orienting device in certain situations, particularly sales letters. That personal link could be a person the two of you know, an event the two of you took part in, or a conversation the two of you had not long before you're writing.

I spoke yesterday with Charlie Blake, who suggested I get in touch with you about a new service our company is offering.

I'm happy we had a chance to talk this morning, and I'm delighted you are interested in attending our conference.

3. *Gain sympathy.*

The obvious time to gain sympathy in your Orienting paragraph is when you're writing to someone you need to mollify. The cardinal rule in such a situation is to address the anger first, before you go any further.

I'm writing to tell you *how sorry I was* to hear of the troubles you had last week with our production staff and to offer some suggestions on how we might avoid these troubles in the future.

First of all, Paul, I want to apologize for flying off the handle this afternoon. I didn't have all the facts at my disposal and I realize now that you were not to blame.

Some Final Thoughts on ORSON

The ORSON model in and of itself won't guarantee that the memos you write will be clear, concise, and, when necessary, convincing. But it will go a long way toward simplifying the process you go through to write business correspondence. The fact that you now have a specific objective for each section of your letter or memo helps to order your thinking. You're able to concentrate on one thing at a time, knowing that when everything is put together, it's all going to work.

ORSON is a particularly useful technique when you're dictating, and for the same reason: it offers a clear target for each individual section of your letter or memo.

8 | The Key to Stronger Paragraphs

The ORSON model is a useful tool for organizing the sequence of information in the typical business document, but it is of limited value when it comes to organizing material within individual paragraphs. Indeed, the carpentry that underlies strong, cohesive paragraphs—in any kind of writing—has proven to be one of the more elusive aspects of writing to pattern. Yes, there are some typical paragraph structures that can serve as models (and most books on basic composition cover these basic models), but the shape a paragraph must ultimately take—the manner in which the information is sequenced and paced—is always determined by the nature of the material you're working with and by what you're trying to accomplish. In a magazine advertisement, a paragraph might consist of a single word. In a *New Yorker* essay, it could run the better part of a page.

One thing I *do* know, however. All well-written paragraphs, regardless of the medium and regardless of the subject, share at least two important qualities. First, the meaning of the paragraph is always *clear:* regardless of how much information the paragraph is conveying, you don't have to be psychic to relate all of it to a central thought or, as I like to call it, Umbrella

Thought—a thought that embraces all the individual ideas within the paragraph. Second, the flow from one sentence to another within the paragraph is reasonably smooth: regardless of how many sentences there are, you don't need a Hammond atlas to follow the flow of information.

That well-written paragraphs share these two qualities is no surprise when you consider that they are precisely what readers *need* if the basic requirements of reading are to be met—that is, if readers are to grasp meaning and follow the flow of information. What's surprising, however, is how frequently these two qualities are conspicuously absent from so much of what you read, especially in business. To illustrate my point, let's compare two paragraphs that deal with essentially the same subject but not with the same degree of clarity.

Currently, there is a $15 fine for anyone parking in a handicapped space without a proper sticker. The police must enforce this fine by handing out tickets. A lot of shopping centers do not have a policeman on duty all the time. Handing out tickets becomes a random process, and a person's chances of being caught in a handicapped spot are cut down. A policeman should be assigned to all major shopping centers on a daily basis. A separate parking area, with a separate store entrance, should be provided for handicapped individuals. It would cut down on the fighting over parking spaces, especially if the designated areas were on the side.

As in Teen Center example given in Chapter 6, there is nothing grammatically *wrong* with this paragraph. Yet, it doesn't *read* well. We're not really sure, as we're reading it (or even after we've finished it), what the paragraph really *means,* other than that it has something to do with parking spaces for the handicapped.

Consider the revision:

If we're serious about preserving the rights of the handicapped, we need to do a better job of enforcing the rules that prohibit parking spaces reserved for the handicapped, particularly in shopping centers. Currently, for instance, the only penalty you receive if you park illegally in a shopping center parking space for the handicapped is a $15 fine, and because police are rarely on duty in a shopping center, people who park in these spaces are rarely caught. So, if we're going to make it easier for the handicapped, a policeman needs to be assigned to shopping centers on a daily basis. And if this practice doesn't work, then we need to provide a separate parking lot with a separate store entrance for handicapped individuals alone.

Two principles underlie this revision.

First, I've given the revision an Umbrella Thought—*the need to enforce the parking laws that are meant to benefit the handicapped.* As you'll notice, each sentence in the revised paragraph conveys essentially that same thought, albeit in different ways.

Second, I've linked the sentences with a number of words and phrases (*for instance, so, and,* etc.) that serve to smooth out the ride as you read through the paragraph. I'll get to the sentence-building technique that underlies these linking words and phrases in the next chapter, but let's look at another pair of examples:

The corporate-jet industry is growing at a fast rate. The industry concept, developed by the late Bill Lear, was the beginning of the corporate-owned jet. The traveling businessman needed a form of transportation to suit a hectic schedule. Many corporations are buying small business jets almost as fast as they're being produced. Bill Lear's company is the leader of the field.

Thanks to the late Bill Lear, the corporate-jet industry is growing at a fast rate. It was Lear who first recognized that traveling businessmen needed a form of transportation designed to suit their hectic schedules and Lear who developed the first corporate jet. Today, corporate jets are being bought almost as fast as they're being produced, and it is no surprise that Lear's company is the leader of the field.

Here again we have one paragraph—the first—that peppers us with with a succession of thoughts that are vaguely related but make no real sense. Here again, as we read this paragraph, we have trouble deciding what, in fact, the paragraph is about. Is it about Bill Lear, corporate jets, a fast-growing industry?

Here again, though, we've corrected the problem by using two techniques: we've made the paragraph *about* Bill Lear and his role in the corporate-jet industry, and we've made sure (by using Lear as the vehicle throughout the paragraph) that each thought in that paragraph conveys the same idea.

Not every paragraph, of course, will lend itself to this pattern. Paragraphs in which you are narrating a sequence of events, for instance, don't usually need special words or phrases to produce cohesion: the natural flow of the material is cohesive in and of itself. Here's an example of one such paragraph from *Newsweek:*

On a sunny morning last week three Israelis from Jerusalem's unofficial liaison office in Lebanon set out on a sightseeing tour. From a town just north of Beirut they headed by car for Byblos, an ancient Phoenician port 20 miles up the coast. They wore civilian clothes but carried small arms for protection. Apparently they missed a turn; suddenly they found themselves approaching a Syrian Army checkpoint. They made a frantic U-turn. Then the Syrians opened fire. The Israelis sprinted back to a Lebanese Army checkpoint. But with Syrian soldiers moving in on all sides, the Lebanese officer in charge agreed to transfer the three men to a Lebanese garrison in Syrian-held territory. There, Syrian troops closed in again, seized the Israelis, and whisked them off in a helicopter to Damascus.

No such *inherent* logic, however, is found in the following paragraph from a student paper. And the writer, unfortunately, hasn't done much to *establish* any logic.

Digesting the seed catalog's abundant offerings can be a pleasure in itself. As you peruse the vegetarian's delights, you plan that this year's garden will be continuously productive. The temptation to order five varieties of squash for a family of two should be suppressed, but indulge yourself and try something unfamiliar. That spaghetti squash or burpless cuke might be just what you need in mid-July.

The trouble with this paragraph begins in the third sentence. Until that point, the paragraph appears to be about the pleasures of reading through a seed catalog and planning a garden. The third sentence, however, introduces an entirely *new* thought—the necessity of suppressing the temptation to overorder—and doesn't adequately prepare us for the change.

This is a classic—and all too familiar—case of a paragraph without a clear Umbrella Thought. As we read the paragraph, we *expect* the third sentence to relate to the first two. So, when we come across an unrelated thought, it confuses us; we don't know what to do with it.

Consider the revision, in which we introduce the idea of "being careful" in the first sentence, and carry the idea throughout the rest of the paragraph.

Digesting the seed catalog's abundant offerings can be a pleasure in itself, but you have to be careful not to let yourself be carried away. Resist the temptation, as you peruse the vegetarian's delights in the catalog, to envision a garden that contains *everything*. It's unlikely, for instance, that you'll have a need for *five* varieties of squash. On the other hand, don't deny yourself the pleasure of adventure. For variety, consider a spaghetti squash or a burpless cuke.

Writing out the Umbrella Thought in the first (or, in some cases, the second or third) sentence of a paragraph is a technique I call the Umbrella Statement (you may know it as the topic sentence), and it's something nearly everybody learns to do in grade school, but, for some reason, promptly forgets soon thereafter. Too bad. Umbrella Statements, which I discuss at length in *How to Write Like a Pro,* represent one of the best ways to make certain your readers will grasp—and hold on to—the meaning of your paragraphs. If you don't believe me, get hold of *Time* or *Newsweek* or any major magazine and take note of how often the first sentence in a paragraph will be an Umbrella Statement.

The reason you find so many Umbrella Statements in these magazines is simple: Umbrella Statements simplify and speed up the reading experience. The sooner you know as a reader what the paragraph is about, the easier it becomes for you to tie together the rest of the information in the paragraph. You don't need to fight through the words to derive meaning. You can sit back and enjoy the ride. Read the following paragraph, taken from a piece in *New York* magazine about Tiffany's that was written by Anthony Haden-Guest, and you'll see a classic illustration of this principle at work. Notice how every sentence from the second sentence on repeats the thought expressed in the Umbrella Statement.

But Tiffany is not a posh department store like, say, Bergdorf Goodman. You can't get cashmeres or sugared cashews at Tiffany. Tiffany is the place for durables, things about-the-house, but things that are accessories rather in the way that jewels are. The Tiffany customer is well-to-do and not much of a bargain-hunter. According to an analysis by Morgan Stanley & Company, the median income of the Tiffany customer is $74,000, and that customer "is not motivated by price consideration in making purchases."

Three more sets of examples before we go on. Here again you'll be looking first at a paragraph that is grammatically correct but doesn't hold together, and then at a revision that corrects the problem by starting the paragraph with an Umbrella Statement and by packaging the rest of the sentences so that they fit within a single Umbrella Thought.

Example 1:

January and February of this year were two of the worst months in our company's history. Our sales were off more than 20%, and, because of salary increases, our expenses actually rose. I'm happy to report that we've had one of our most successful years. From March to July, we managed to break even. The months from August through December saw a very sharp increase in sales.

The problem with this paragraph is obvious. The first two sentences are laden with doom and gloom. Then, in the third sentence, we're told that things couldn't be rosier. A puzzlement. The writer, of course, knew all along that he had good news to share but didn't realize, apparently, that the one thing readers can't read is minds.

The Umbrellaized revision:

I'm happy to report that in spite of a very slow start, we've had one of our most successful years. True, January and February were two of the worst months in our company's history, and the best we could do from March to July was to break even. The success we enjoyed from August through December, however, more than made up for the slow start. Our sales during this period rose sharply.

Similar information, but a different—and clearer—package, keyed by an Umbrella Statement, which sets up the rest of the information in the paragraph.

Example 2:

With a lack of navigational aids that will result from the new government plan, there will be more boating accidents, thus leading to the necessity for more Coast Guard Patrols. More state and local dollars would have to be spent on police and rescue teams. Raising state and local boat taxes is not the answer for more revenue because there is no easy, enforceable means of stopping people from registering their boats out of state, where taxes would be lower. That is a severe problem which has been plaguing Connecticut tax collectors for years. Another possible cost hike would be insurance rates because people would be more likely to have a boating accident.

This paragraph starts out as if it were going to be about the increase of boating accidents that's likely to occur in light of the new government plan to reduce navigational aids. The second sentence, however, introduces a slightly different thought—the additional money that the plan is likely to cost. The third sentence introduces still another thought: the problem of enforcing proper boat registration. The final sentence leads us back to the idea of more money, by which time, alas, it's too late. We're hopelessly lost.

The Umbrellaized revision:

The new federal government plan to reduce navigational aids isn't going to save money, as its supporters claim; it will end up costing money. With a lack of navigational aids, there will be more boating accidents, thus leading to the necessity for more Coast Guard Patrols and more state and local tax dollars for police and rescue teams. (And even if local and state taxes were raised, incidentally, it's unlikely that there would be enough money to support the additional rescue efforts. That's because there is no easy and enforceable means of stopping people from registering their boats out of state, where taxes would be lower.) Let's not forget, either, that an increase in boating accidents will lead to an increase in insurance rates.

Notice that you find out exactly what this paragraph is about in the first sentence. Notice, too, that each of the subsequent sentences, with the exception of the third and fourth (which

I've parenthesized) is essentially a restatement of the same thought. Why the parenthesis? Why indeed! It tells the reader that the information within the parenthesis is interesting but only marginally related to the Umbrella Thought.

Example 3:

What makes us grown-up, anyway? Is it wearing eye shadow or bikini bathing suits? Frankly, I do both but not at the same time. Am I then half mature? This maturity or change process is continuing inside ourselves and we vent it differently to meet the situation. Every generation experiences it. We all relinquish childhood treasures. Unfortunately, sometimes these treasures are human beings. We feel that we outgrow our relationships with people. The common base of going to bed early, watching Disney World and playing hopscotch at recess held us together as a unity in grade school. What happens in Jr. high when a few stay up to watch Johnny Carson or leave the hopscotch game to kiss behind the trees on the playground? What happened?

This paragraph, from a personal essay written by one of my Fairfield University students, has some nice insights but it fails because the writer didn't give the insights a clear enough umbrella. In the revision that follows, the Umbrella Statement appears not at the beginning but as the third sentence—early enough, however, to establish a framework for the remainder of the paragraph. Yes, I've made some other changes: I've parenthesized one of sentences and added some phrases. But the changes, as you'll see, are all logical and designed to produce cohesion in this paragraph.

The revision:

What makes us grown-up, anyway? Is it wearing eye shadow or bikini bathing suits? (I do both but not at the same time. Am I then half mature?) The answer, of course, is that maturity isn't something external: it's a process that continues inside ourselves as we grow older, and it is something that carries with it a sense of loss. For as we become more grown up, we relinquish childhood treasures—treasures that unfortunately can be human beings. In short, we outgrow people. The things we shared in grammar school—going to bed early, watching Disney World and playing hopscotch at recess—no longer hold us together when we move into junior high, when a few of us begin staying up to watch Johnny Carson or leave the hopscotch game to kiss behind the trees on the playground.

Putting Umbrellaizing to Work

Umbrellaizing can be an elusive concept to put into practice. That's because it embraces both the stylistic and conceptual aspects of writing. The Umbrella Statement, for instance, is pretty much a stylistic technique, as are the three techniques we'll be looking at in the next chapter: Who-Do Writing, Signposting, and Looping Back. But unless the ideas within the paragraph are unified enough to produce an easily identifiable Umbrella Thought, none of these techniques will assure you a cohesively written paragraph. That's where the conceptual part comes in. It's your job, as a writer, to organize the thoughts within the paragraph in way that's logical to the reader.

I can't *teach* you logic, but I can offer a few suggestions that will help you supply your own logic.

- Get into the habit of deciding, *before you start to write a paragraph,* what Umbrella Thought you want that paragraph to convey. You should be able to summarize the thought in a few words. In the case of the paragraph that opened this section, for instance, the Umbrella Thought is "Umbrellaizing can be elusive." The paragraph works (I think) because each of the succeeding sentences falls within that Umbrella Thought.

- If you have trouble expressing the Umbrella Thought in a few words, chances are you haven't yet clarified in your own mind what thought you're trying to get across. Step back and rethink your approach. If you find you have more than one point to get across, see if you can come up with an Umbrella Thought that incorporates the many different ideas. If this proves impossible, consider the possibility of separating ideas so that each paragraph has a new thought.

- Once you've settled upon an Umbrella Thought, see if it makes sense to start the paragraph with an Umbrella Statement. It won't always be practical. When the paragraph is very short, or when the meaning of the paragraph is obvious, it generally doesn't need an Umbrella Statement. Generally speaking, however, Umbrella Statements are *underused* in most day-to-day writing.

- If you're going to include information in the paragraph that deviates from the Umbrella Thought, let your reader know, with words and phrases to that effect or by setting these ideas off in parentheses, that you're sidetracking, and keep these diversions as *brief* as possible.

Let me conclude this discussion with with an analogy that might put the Umbrellaizing concept in clearer perspective. Writing, in the broadest sense, can be likened to taking a reader on a trip, with the function of each paragraph to advance the reader closer to the destination. If, as a writer, you know ahead of time where you want each paragraph to take your reader (which assumes, of course, that you know the *overall* destination), each sentence within the paragraph simply represents one leg of that journey. As with all trips, there are different ways of getting there and plenty of opportunities for side trips. And while it's okay now and then to stray from the main route, never stray so far that your reader won't be able to find his way back quickly and easily.

9 | How to Put More Life into Your Sentences

Simplicity is to writing instruction what motherhood is to political rhetoric: you can never go wrong preaching its virtues. Odd, then, that when you read most business or technical correspondence or even most school papers, simplicity turns out to be the one thing, above all, that is conspicuously lacking.

There are two fundamental reasons for this paradox. First, old habits die hard. So unless you were fortunate enough to have one of those rare English teachers who *encouraged* you to write in a clean, crisp style, you may have grown up believing that the more convoluted your writing style, the more respect you'd command as a writer. Second, most people, even if they *wanted* to write more simply, don't know *how* to do it—don't know how, that is, to write simply yet in a style that isn't too choppy or doesn't read like a day in the life of Dick and Jane.

If you are going to learn to write in a simpler, more vigorous, and livelier style—and I think you *should*—you're going to have to do two things: one, recognize that there's a difference between writing *simply* and writing *simplistically;* and, two, learn some techniques that will enable you to combine simplicity with flow. In this chapter, we'll look into three such techniques, which I call Who-Do Writing, Signposting, and Looping Back.

Who-Do Writing

Let's begin our discussion of the technique I call Who-Do Writing by comparing two paragraphs. The first is a doctored version of a paragraph that appeared not long ago on the editorial page of *The New York Times*. The second is the way the paragraph actually appeared.

Even experiments with photographic coverage where both sides in a trial give consent have been barred by the new report of the Judicial Conference. The adverse psychological effects on jurors, lawyers, and presiding judges have been cited. Courtroom behavior ranging "from encouraging histrionics to inhibition" have been suggested as effects, and worry has been expressed about a "great potential for miseducation and presentation of distorted images." Only meager support for these conclusions has been offered by this report. The experience in forty-one states, which suggests that cameras in court can often enhance justice and increase public understanding, has been ignored.

The new report of the Judicial Conference, however, bars even experiments with photographic coverage, and even where both sides in a trial give consent. It speaks of "potential" adverse psychological effects on jurors, lawyers, and presiding judges. It simply assumes effects on courtroom behavior that range "from encouraging histrionics to inhibition" and worries about a "great potential for miseducation and presentation of distorted images." But the report offers only meager support for those conclusions. It ignores the experience in forty-one states, which suggests that cameras in court can often enhance justice and increase public understanding.

Chances are, you found the second of these paragraphs a good deal easier to read than the first, and there's a logical reason. In the second paragraph, the subject of the sentence and the main verb in each of the sentences are *next to one another* and appear *at or near the beginning* of the sentence. Not so in the first paragraph.

This particular pattern, in which the subject—the Who—and main verb—the Do—of a sentence appear together and early in the sentence, occurs over and over in writing that reads quickly and and easily, and no wonder. The sooner in a sentence your reader is able to put together the subject of the main thought (the Who) and the action (the Do), the easier it's going be for the reader to grasp the thought, and the more quickly the reader will be able to navigate the rest of the sentence.

Let's look at another example, this time a paragraph from the introduction to *On Language* (Avon, 1981), by William Safire, *The New York Times* columnist. Notice that in almost every sentence you can identify the Who of the sentence and the Do of the sentence almost immediately.

English is a stretch language. One size fits all. That does not mean anything goes; in most instances, anything does not go. But the language, as it changes, conforms itself to special groups and occasions. There is a time for dialect, a place for slang, an occasion for literary form. What is correct on the sports page is out of place on the op-ed page; what is with it on the street may well be without it in the classroom. The spoken language does not have the same standards as the written language—the tune you whistle is not the orchestra's score.

English [Who] *is* [Do] a stretch language. One *size* [Who] *does* [Do] not fit all. *That* [Who] *does* [Do] not mean anything goes; in most instances, *anything* [Who] *does* [Do] not go. But the *language* [Who], as it changes, *conforms* [Do] itself to special groups and occasions. *There* [Who] *is* [Do] a time for dialect, a place for slang, an occasion for literary form. *What is correct on the sports page* [Who] *is* [Do] out of place on the op-ed page; *what is with it on the street* [Who] *may* well *be* [Do] without it in the classroom. The spoken *language* [Who] *does* not *have* [Do] the same standards as the written language—the *tune you whistle* [Who] *is* [Do] not the orchestra's score.

To be sure, there are times when you'll want to deviate intentionally from the Who-Do pattern. If you're raising a hypothetical point (as I'm doing in this sentence), you have no choice but to precede the Who-Do portion of the sentence with an introductory clause that starts with "If." Sometimes, too, you'll want to change the pattern simply to achieve a particular effect. There is a sentence writing technique—it's called the periodic sentence—in which you build suspense by witholding the main clause until well past the middle of the sentence. It's a stagey technique, out of place perhaps in normal business correspondence, but it works well in copywriting. Example: "Three years ago, convinced that there was a need in America for a car that was luxurious but inexpensive, the Arrow Motor company hired a team of designers straight out of MIT."

Generally speaking, however, Who-Do should be the *dominant* pattern in your writing. When you write Who-Do style, you minimize the number of sentences written in the passive voice, in which the *true* Who of the sentence (the person or thing doing the doing) is either missing or assumes a less important role in the sentence as the *object* of the verb. So, instead of this:

A practice is made by management to follow a consultative process of decision-making with field supervisors on key decisions. The possibility of conflict is reduced by this practice. Supervisors are encouraged to take part in the decision-making process.

You would write this:

Management [Who] makes [Do] it a practice to consult field supervisors before making any key decisions. This practice [Who] reduces [Do] the likelihood of conflict between the management and the field. It [Who] also encourages [Do] more supervisors to take part in the decision-making process.

Who-Do Writing also helps keep you from the all-too-common practice of preceding the true meat of your sentence—the main clause—with an introductory subordinate clause so long and rambling that by the time the reader gets to the meat, he's lost. So instead of writing:

Although it has been recognized over the years that one of the ingredients inherent in good management development is a training program that maximizes basic management skills, promotions to higher management have not always been predicated on skills learned in these training programs.

you would write:

We [Who] have recognized [Do] over the years that training basic management skills [Who] is [Do] an essential ingredient in management development. Yet, we [Who] have not always based [Do] promotions to higher management on the skills learned in these programs.

Finally, writing Who-Do style helps to "order" your thinking while you write. It literally forces you to build your sentences around the subject and the action and assures you that the two most important elements of your sentences will never be buried.

Putting Who-Do Writing to Work

To see how Who-Do Writing might work in an actual writing situation, let's compare the following two paragraphs:

Scope Support is a recent concept which emphasizes easy, flexible access to computer-based information. Offering selected portions of indepth information generally available in a large computer system, the innovation, a compact, less technical "user-tailored" approach, is capable of providing immediate feedback on the user's specific problems.

Scope Support is a recent concept which emphasizes easy, flexible access to computer-based information. It offers selected portions of indepth information generally available in a large computer system, and it does so with a compact, less technical "user-tailored" approach that is capable of providing immediate feedback on the user's specific problems.

The two paragraphs begin the same way, but look what happens in the second sentence of each paragraph. In the first paragraph, we deviate from the Who-Do pattern, and look at how confusing the paragraph suddenly becomes. In the second paragraph, because Who-Do Writing obliges us to start the second sentence with the Who, we have no choice but to start the sentence with either *Scope Support* or *It* and to follow with the Do—*offers*. As a result, the thoughts connect more cohesively.

So the key to Who-Do Writing is to keep your focus on the most important elements of the thoughts you're conveying—

the subject and the action—*while* you're writing. If the first sentence of your paragraph reads, "The new report of the Judicial Conference, however, bars even experiments with photographic coverage, and even where both sides in a trial give consent," and your second sentence *also* deals with that same report, your first impulse should be to *begin* that second as the writer did in the example above: "It [Who] speaks [Do] . . ." I find, in fact, that Who-Do Writing acts as a centering device. Whenever I'm struggling to pull my thoughts together in the middle of a paragraph, I simply ask myself, "Who's doing the doing here," and I'm usually able to get myself back on the track.

Signposting: Smoothing Out Who-Do Writing

Who-Do Writing usually produces a writing style that's simple and direct, but the sentence rhythms that result can often be choppy. To see what I mean, read the following paragraph in which the writer is describing a workshop for supervisors:

The workshop will focus on interviewing skills for middle-level supervisors. It will emphasize a strategic approach to interviewing. It will review the factors to be considered in successful interviewing. It will outline a range of interviewing techniques. It will give participants the opportunity to develop responses to a series of questions likely to come up in the interview.

This paragraph reads clearly, but most writers would be uncomfortable with its choppy and monotonous rhythsm. If asked to revise the paragraph, moreover, most people would be likely to write something along the lines of the following:

The workshop will focus on interviewing skills for middle-level supervisors. A strategic approach to interviewing will be emphasized, along with a review of factors to be considered in successful interviewing. A conceptual framework outlining the range of interviewing techniques will be presented. Participants will have the opportunity to develop responses to a series of questions likely to come up in the interview.

We've smoothed out the choppiness, but we've also made the paragraph wordier and tougher to read. Consider now the following revision:

The workshop will focus on interviewing skills for middle-level supervisors. It will emphasize a strategic approach to interviewing and will review the factors to be considered in successful interviewing. It will also outline a range of interviewing techniques, and, finally, will give participants the opportunity to develop responses to a series of questions likely to come up in the interview.

Two techniques allowed us to write Who-Do style but without the monotony and the choppiness of the first example. First, we've changed the first two sentences and the last two sentences of the original from single clause sentences into complex sentences, and by doing so have eliminated the pauses that helped make the first example so choppy. (There isn't much to say about this technique except that it's a cosmetic change and should never be made when it muddies up meaning.) Second, we've added a number of little words—*also, and,* and *finally,* that smooth the flow from one sentence to another. I call these little words Signposts. They indicate how sentences relate to one another and thus serve to "guide" the reader through the paragraph.

You can see the power of Signposting by comparing the following two paragraphs. The original version—the second of the two that follow—was written by novelist, journalist, and screenwriter John Gregory Dunne. The first is my version of the same paragraph in which I deleted all the Signposts that Dunne used. Notice, by the way, that all but one of the sentences in the paragraphs follow the Who-Do model. Notice, too, how much more smoothly the second paragraph reads because of the handful of Signposts.

We were asked to write a picture for Barbra Streisand. We did not think much of the book we had been asked to adapt. We had turned it down twice before Streisand was involved. Such was the lure of Streisand that we were almost able to convince ourselves that she could make this story work. The director encouraged this delusion; he had not liked the book. With the Streisand magic, he said, perhaps we could pull it off.

We were asked to write a picture for Barbra Streisand. *Unfortunately,* we did not think much of the book we had been asked to adapt; we Vad, *in fact,* turned it down twice before Streisand was involved. *But* such was the lure of Streisand that we were almost able to convince ourselves that she could make even this story work. The director encouraged this delusion; he had not liked the book, *either, but* with the Streisand magic, he said, perhaps we could pull it off.

Putting Signposting to Work

To know that certain words, when used strategically, can smooth out Who-Do writing is useful information, but it doesn't solve the problem of how to use these words. Unfortunately, the ability to use Signposts effectively is largely a matter of ''ear'' or ''feel'' or whatever you choose to call the ability that some writers have to smooth out the bumps of clumsy sentences with nothing more than a word of two. Still, there is a logic to using Signposts, and the logic derives from the relationship between the sentences you're connecting. With this logic in mind, I've arbitrarily divided Signposts into two broad categories and have broken down these two categories into five subcategories, based on what each Signpost is meant to do.

The two general categories, and their subcategories, are:

1. **Focus Holders.** Words and phrases that tell your readers to keep their focus on the idea or image they are focusing on at the moment.

> • *Clarifiers.* Words and phrases that tell your reader you're about to clarify an idea you've just introduced. Example:

The machine is semiautomatic. *This means that* once you've fed it the paper, it will do the rest of the work by itself.

> • *Exemplifiers.* Words and phrases that tell the reader

you're about to cite examples or illustrations of an
idea you've just introduced. Example:

There are several different approaches you can take to getting the
information you need. You can ask the person directly, *for instance,* or
try to find out from the person's supervisor.

- *Intensifiers.* Words and phrases that tell the reader
you're about to amend or intensify an idea you've
just introduced. Example:

We've worked extremely hard in this department to meet our dead-
lines. *Indeed,* I know of no other department that has put in as much
overtime.

2. Focus Shifters. Words and phrases that alert the reader to an
imminent focus *shift.*

- *Qualifiers.* Words and phrases that tell the reader
you're about to qualify, contradict, contrast, or
concede an idea. Example:

It's always a good idea to assure your customers that you're sensitive to their problems. Keep in mind, *however,* that there is only a certain amount you yourself can do to solve these problems.

- *Consequentials.* Words and phrases that tell the
reader you're about to show the consequences of
the idea you've just presented. Example:

It's essential that we finish this project on time. *Therefore,* I am asking that all employees work overtime all next week.

The list that follows contains Signposts for each of the five
categories. I recommend that you either transcribe or photocopy the list, keep it by your desk, and get into the habit of
using the words when the situation warrants it. As far as *which*
specific Signpost is best to use when you have a choice of several
in the same category, it ultimately comes down to how each one
sounds. Apart from the fact that I try to vary the phrases, I can't
tell you why I'll use "for instance" in one sentence and "for example" someplace else. It depends on which one seems to fit more
naturally when I read the sentences aloud to myself. In general,
though, I prefer the shorter, crisper Signposts like *yet, still, so,* and
but over the lengthier and more formal Signposts like *in contrast,*

nevertheless, consequently, and *however.* A funny thing about those shorter, punchier Signposts: they do the job, but you don't really notice they're there until you look back and count noses.

Something else, too. Signposts are like exotic cooking spices: best used in moderation. If you overuse Signposts, you will end up impeding, not enhancing, the flow of your material. Worse, your writing will sound as though it were inspired by every pretentious and overblown commencement speech you've ever attended. How many signposts are too many? Well, not long ago I did a random check of some nicely done professional articles that I keep in a file near my desk and found an average of three or four Signposts for each good sized (eight or nine sentences) paragraph. This would break down to about one Signpost for every three sentences, which seems to be a reasonable guideline. Stay within that guideline and you'll keep out of trouble.

Focus Holders

Clarifiers

What this means is
I mean
To understand this, you must
The point is this
I'm talking about
This means that
That is to say
The reason is

Exemplifiers

For example
To illustrate
For instance
First of all
To begin with
Take, for example,

For one thing
Consider
In the first place

Intensifiers

And
What's more
In addition
Moreover
Then, too,
Also
Even more
There's more
In fact
Worse yet
As well
Either
By the same token
Indeed
And that's not all
Further
Furthermore
Beyond this
Apart from this
Not only . . . but also
The fact is
Better still
Yet another

Focus Shifters

Qualifiers

But
Although
On the other hand

Even so
However
Then again
By way of contrast
Still
Yet
To the contrary
On the other hand
Nevertheless
Even though
Nonetheless
All the same
No matter
True
Granted
In spite of
Instead
Either

Consequentials

Consequently
So
Hence
Thus
Because of this
Then
As a result
Accordingly
Therefore

Where to Place the Signpost

One more word about Signposts before we move on. Signposts don't necessarily have to come at the *beginning* of a sentence. Very often, in fact, your sentences will read more smoothly if you insert the signpost after the first phrase.

Instead of:

We had hoped to finish the project by early June. However, we now find that shipping delays have forced us to alter the schedule.

this:

We had hoped to finish the project by early June. We now find, however, that shipping delays have forced us to alter the schedule.

Instead of:

The new promotion is going much better than we figured. For instance, in Chicago sales are up by 30 percent.

this:

The new promotion is going much better than we figured. In Chicago, for instance, sales are up by 30 percent.

Looping Back

The last of the sentence-writing patterns I want to talk about in this chapter produces a quality that's frequently lacking in the writing of nonprofessionals who are otherwise able to present their information in a reasonably simple and well-organized fashion: a cohesive flow from thought to thought. Signposting helps produce this cohesion, but the technique that *assures* this cohesiveness is something I call Looping Back. Here, again, the best way to appreciate what the technique can contribute is to read two versions of a paragraph, only one of which uses it.

Attached is the latest labor analysis report. We need to find ways to reduce overtime expenditures because the costs are 20 percent higher than last year. An analysis of overtime costs over the past six months is included in the report. Recommendations are requested on how to cut back.

Attached is the latest labor analysis report. Included in it is an analysis of overtime costs over the six months. Because these costs are 20

percent higher than last year, I'd like you to make some recommendations on how we can reduce overtime expenditues.

You probably found the first of these two paragraphs more
disjointed than the second: it's tough to move from sentence to
sentence. Not so in the second paragraph, and that's because of
certain phrases in that paragraph whose function is direct your
focus to thoughts introduced in the previous sentence. The
phrase *in it* in the second sentence of the second paragraph, for
instance, directs your focus—i.e., loops back—to *labor report* in
the first sentence. The word *costs* in the third sentence loops
back to *costs* in the second sentence.

What Looping Back does, in other words, is help prevent
that brief but usually disruptive moment when the reader is
taking in information but isn't sure of what to do with it.

Look at the following two sentences:

In addition to the program under consideration, we are presently
looking into a new procedure tailored to the needs of Corporate Human Resources. The Tracking Interview will evaluate the progress of
recent hires in all locations in areas of salary, status, job level, and so
forth.

The problem here is connecting the Tracking Interview to
"new procedure." The writer, presumably, already knows the
connection, but the reader has no way of making the same connection. If you're reading this material for the first time, the
Tracking Interview is simply a new piece of information. It's
not until you finish the sentence that you know enough to connect the two phrases.

Let's correct the problem by Looping Back.

In addition to the program under consideration, we are now looking
into a new procedure tailored to the needs of Corporate Human Resources. It [the new procedure] will have the capability—by means of
something known as the Tracking Interview—to evaluate the progress of recent hires at all locations in areas of salary, status, job level,
and so forth.

What we've done here is to eliminate any chance of ambiguity or confusion. By starting the second sentence with *it*, we

keep the reader's focus on the procedure. And because we introduce the idea of the Tracking Interview *after* we've talked
about capability, the reader doesn't have to scramble to figure
out what it all means.

The principle behind Looping Back, then, is this: whenever
the connection between two sentences in a paragraph isn't obvious (as it is, say, in paragraphs in which you are narrating a
series of events that follow a logical chronological sequence),
you need to Loop Back either directly (by repeating the word or
phrase mentioned in the previous sentence or with an indefinite
pronoun), or indirectly (through a word or phrase that is close
enough in meaning to the previous focal meaning to make the
connection an easy one).

Let's look at an example from John Leonard's essay called
"Civility" (*Private Lives in the Imperial City,* Ballantine, New
York, 1976) the better to see both types of Looping Back:

When the news came last week that the English novelist Paul Scott
had died, I was sorting books. I should have begun sorting my books
[direct]—categorizing, alphabetizing, in some cases burning—twenty
years ago but I've pretended instead to subscribe to a principle of serendipity. That is, if I didn't know where to find the particular book I
wanted when I went to look I would find a different, better book, [in-
direct,because it relates to the idea of *serendipity*] a book I hadn't
thought of. This principle of serendipity [direct] is opposed to the
principle of the study of ablations. An ablation [direct] is a tumor or
diseased organ, removed by surgery.

Basic Principles of Looping Back

Here are three principles to keep in mind that will
help you use the Looping Back technique more effectively:

1. Use one of the focal points of the previous sentence as the Looping Back cue.

Original:

The Broadway theater honors its outstanding members each year with the Tony Awards ceremony. Sunday, June 7, is the date.

Revision:

The Broadway theater honors its outstanding members each year with the Tony Awards ceremony. *This year's* ceremony will be held on Sunday, June 7.

2. Make sure any pronoun early in a sentence has an easy-to-recognize antecedent.

Original:

Events over the past several weeks have pointed up the need to change some of our policies. They are self-evident.

Revision:

Events over the past several weeks have pointed up the need to change some of our policies. *The policies* that need changing are self-evident.

3. Don't hesitate to repeat a word if it will enhance the cohesiveness of a passage.

Original:

The new plastic molds pose two problems. Their lack of sufficient capacity is one difficulty. The second obstacle is that they produce a hard, brittle surface.

Revision:

The new plastic molds pose two problems. *Problem* number one is that they lack sufficient capacity. *Problem* number two is that they produce a hard, brittle surface.

If the last of the three examples above strikes an unsettling chord, it may be that you've been conditioned to avoid repetition and to use synonyms instead. Chances are, you own a *Roget's Thesaurus*. I have nothing against Roget, but it's time you shed this cumbersome restraint. Accomplished professional writers are constantly repeating the same words—or, to be more explicit, accomplished professionals do not change words arbitrarily, for the pure sake of changing them. To prove my point, look at these two versions of a paragraph from Michael Korda's book *Success*. (Random House, 1977). The first paragraph reads the way Korda wrote it. The second reads the way it might have read if Korda had gone out of his way to be more varied in his word choice.

One thing is basic: power people have their shoes polished, or do it themselves. In all shoe-wearing cultures, and in every age, a dirty shoe is a sign of weakness. Latin American gentlemen of the old school spend hours sitting in the streets having their shoes shined, and the best place to see important people lined up is at the shoeshine stand in any big office building at about nine in the morning. Many powerful people have a second shoeshine after lunch, when the shoeshine man makes his afternoon visit to their offices to restore the morning's gloss. At night, when they go home, they can afford to get their shoes dusty and scuffed, since they are leaving the world of power. This explains why there are no shoeshine stands at commuter stations, and very few open after five—nobody needs a shine on the way home.

One thing is basic: power people have their shoes polished, or do it themselves. In all foot-apparel-wearing cultures, and in every age, a dirty covering over the lower extremity of the leg is a sign of weakness. Latin American gentlemen of the old school spend hours sitting in the streets having them gone over, and the best place to see important people lined up is at the gleam stand in any big office building at about nine in the morning. Many powerful people have a second cleaning and polishing after lunch, when the purveyor of neater footwear makes his afternoon visit to their offices to restore the morning's gloss. At night, when they go home, they can afford to get their footgear dusty and scuffed, since they are leaving the world of power. This explains why there are no shoeshine stands at commuter stations, and very few open after five—nobody needs a shine on the way home.

Some Final Thoughts

What keeping your eye on the ball, bending your knees, and following through are to hitting a tennis ball, Who-Do Writing, Signposting, and Looping Back are to writing. They represent the basic patterns of effective writing, and once you get accustomed to using them, you'll find they not only produce clear, concise writing but go a long way toward reducing the amount of time it takes you to write.

Let me warn you, though, against trying to incorporate these techniques into your writing repertoire too quickly. Keep in mind that if these techniques are to work for you, they must become *built-in* patterns, and the process of programming yourself to write in these patterns could take time.

My suggestion is that you don't try to express your thoughts in these patterns in your first draft, but that you use Who-Do Writing, Signposting, and Looping Back as revising techniques. Eventually, after you've used the techniques often enough, they will gradually become a more fixed part of your writing approach, and you won't have to *think* about using them: the words will simply manifest themselves in that form. So, give the process time, and don't make your writing any *more* painful by trying to jam something inside your brain before your brain is receptive to the invasion.

10 | Sentence Surgery: How to Be Your Own Editor

A few years ago I developed an almost foolproof system of editing—or so I thought at the time. It was called the CBS system of editing and it put forth a carefully sequenced series of techniques that fell into no fewer than three different categories: clarity (C), brevity (B), and sharpness (S), the last category of which, in case you're wondering, related to how interesting or engagingly the piece read. My system seemed marvelously logical—simple yet effective—and I couldn't have been more pleased at having come up with so ingenious an approach to an aspect of writing that has long proven so troublesome to so many people. There was only one problem: the system didn't work.

That's not quite true. The system *did* work, and rather well for some of my students. The problem, though, was that my "successes" by and large were with people who were *already* reasonably adept at editing—people who really didn't need me help them read through a manuscript (their own or somebody else's), identify the problem areas, and then make the needed changes with surgical dispatch.

When it came to the majority of my students, however, my

system produced mainly frustration. It wasn't that people couldn't understand the system or couldn't see for themselves how much more clearly, concisely, and smoothly their sentences read after they'd applied the techniques to the rougher edges of their manuscripts. The problem was getting them to recognize the rough edges in the first place. Most people, I now realize, aren't all that anxious to seek out the rough edges in documents they figure they've finished writing, and even if they *are* anxious to root out the imperfections, they're not really sure of what they should be looking for. My system didn't take this factor into account. I made the mistake of assuming that most people are as compulsive about their writing as I am—which they are not, and which is why the system didn't work. I might just as well have been teaching a generation of doctors how to treat an illness they didn't know how to diagnose.

Suffice it to say, I no longer use the system in my seminars. And while I haven't given up entirely on the idea of systematizing the editing process, I now recognize that teaching people how to edit efficiently is as formidable a challenge as teaching people how to manage all the other aspects of the writing process. Here are some of the reasons:

• Like the composing aspect of writing, editing embraces not one but several cognitive skills. For starters, you need to be detail-oriented enough to proofread accurately—to spot misspellings and word omissions, etc.—but not *so* detail-oriented that you can't detect and correct shortcomings relating to the overall intent of the writing. It's important, too, to know enough about grammar that you don't have to call a cerebral summit meeting or riffle through *Fowler's English Usage* any time there's a question about where to stick a comma.

Most important, though, the ability to edit effectively presupposes a fairly well-developed writing "ear." You need to be able to sense (and *sense* is the best word I can think of to describe what I'm talking about) when your ideas aren't jelling or when your sentences are likely to produce too bumpy a ride for your readers. And not only do you need to be able to *sense* these things, you need to be able to perform the corrective surgery without tearing down and rebuilding entire paragraphs. If you excel at any *one* of these faculties, you have a right to be proud. If you excelled at *all* of them, I don't think you'd be reading this book.

• Editing requires an adversarial mind set—an *a priori* assumption that everything you edit is guilty until proven innocent. Adopting so truculent a stance can be difficult enough when you're editing somebody else's material (particularly if you're a tolerant person by nature), but acting as your own editor is like serving as the judge at your own inquisition. The problem isn't just the natural tendency to look upon your writing as a reflection and extension of *you;* it is also a matter of perspective. How can you be absolutely certain, for instance, that what makes perfectly good sense to you will make perfectly good sense to your readers? How can you tell if a word or phrase that seems original or clever to you won't strike your readers as being . . . well, too cutesy, or hackneyed, or labored?

The answer, of course, is that you *can't* tell; the best you can do is make intelligent guesses based on your experience and the standards unique to your particular writing situation. All of which introduces perhaps the thorniest aspect of editing: the fact that once you get past the more obvious problems of ambiguity and usage, deciding what does and doesn't read well usually depends on the situation and, in many instances, comes down to nothing more than a matter of personal taste: what happens to *sound* good to you.

• Editing, if done properly, takes time and in some respects requires an even more intense level of concentration than composing and revising. Even a task as seemingly rudimentary as making absolutely certain that there are no typos and no misspellings on a one-page letter can take several minutes, and you have to give it your full attention or something will invariably slip by. Once you get into the more complicated aspects of editing—substituting words and reshaping sentences, the time and concentration requirements escalate. If your standards are extremely high, there is never *enough* time. Talk to magazine editors. They'll tell you that they often spend more time *editing* a piece than it took the writer to research and write it.

I make these observations not to discourage you from developing specific skills that will improve your ability to edit your own material, but only to caution you against underestimating the difficulty—and the importance—of careful editing. Editing isn't simply a relaxing epilogue to writing—a last minute whiz-through just to make to make sure you've crossed your t's and dotted your i's. On the contrary, editing is as critical to the success of your writing objective as everything you've done prior to the point of editing. What's more, the more adept you become at editing, the easier you will have made it for yourself during the earlier stages of writing. Confident that you'll be able to mop up whatever verbal debris you've left behind as you've been composing and revising, you won't have to strive for perfection too early in the process and so can use your mental energy more strategically and more efficiently. It's a little like being the manager of a baseball team blessed with a terrific bullpen. You tell your starting pitchers to go out, throw hard, and not worry about going the nine.

So even though I have no specific editing system to offer you in this chapter, I have some observations and suggestions about the editing process itself, as well some specific techniques that should help you approach editing in a more systematic—and productive—manner.

Making Things Easier for Yourself

In at least one key respect, editing is no different from the other elements of writing I've been talking about throughout this book. Its cognitive demands apart, there are a number of purely practical steps you can take to make the process go a little more smoothly for you. Here are some of the most important of these steps.

1. *Be sure the document is ready to be edited.*

Difficult though it is to segment the writing process into truly distinct stages, try to keep editing a process that's *separate* from revising—never mind that the kinds of changes you make when you edit (clearing up ambiguity, substituting words, tightening sentences, etc.) are similar to the changes you make when you revise.

The difference lies in the scope of your changes. The improvements you make during editing ought to be primarily cosmetic, not structural, which means you should be able to make your corrections in pencil or pen, noting them in the margins or in between the lines. This limitation, of course, means that the document has to be reasonably finished before you start to edit: the thoughts or information reasonably complete, the structure and organization reasonably solid, and the writing clear enough, at any rate, so that a reader can at least absorb the gist of the message without being tested too severely.

Trying to edit a piece that isn't yet ripe for editing can create grief for you in a number of different ways. What it costs you mostly, though, is time. Polishing a phrase that isn't conveying the idea it's supposed to convey is like applying an extra coat of paint to a ceiling beam that's likely to give way the next time somebody slams a door. Dressing up a sentence that shouldn't have been written in the first place is like sandpapering a wall that somebody is going to rip out that same day. It's bad verbal carpentry.

2. *Prepare each draft to be edited in a form that lends itself to easy corrections.*

To edit efficiently, you need working space: room to write in your changes. If you work with a word processor, of course, no problem; you edit on the screen (although more and more users of word processors are finding that it's better to do the actual editing on hard copy and then transcribe the changes to the screen). If you're typing or writing longhand, on the other hand, leave yourself plenty of space—between each line and in the margins—in which to make your additions or corrections. What's more, as basic as the advice may seem, use a fine-tipped pen or freshly sharpened pencil to write in your changes, and do your best to keep each manuscript as neat as possible. The more scrawlings on the page, the tougher it is to make intelligent judgments.

3. Put "distance" between yourself and the document you're editing.

As I've already emphasized, there are easier things to be than the judge and jury of your own writing, but there are nonetheless a few things you can do to keep your biases in reasonable check. Time is probably your staunchest ally in this regard. The longer you can wait between the moment you've completed your "finished" version and the moment you begin editing, the more objectivity you're likely to bring to the enterprise.

How much time is ideal? It depends entirely on how long or complicated the document is, how polished it has to be to accomplish its objective, and how much time you can afford to wait. Generally, though, the longer the better. If you can hold off for a day or two (or, better still, even longer), do so. If a day or two is impractical, give yourself a few hours. At the very least, take a short break between the time you finish the "writing" part of the task and the "editing" part. Take the manuscript to another room, or another *part* of the room you normally work in (tough, I admit, if you write with a processor, unless you edit on hard copy.) Do anything to give yourself some *distance*. Gay Talese, it might interest you to know, believes so strongly in the principle of distancing in editing that he has occasionally tacked pages of his manuscript on one wall of his office, and has read it from the other end of the office, peering at it through a pair of binoculars.

4. *Set priorities*.

Some professional writers, particularly writers of poetry and short stories, think nothing of rewriting and rewriting and rewriting the same paragraph over and over and over. That's part of the challenge and fun of what they do. This is fine if you have the time for such linguistic indulgences, but not so fine if, like most people, you aren't being paid to turn out lyrical prose.

I can't tell you how much time to spend on editing, but however much time you spend, I urge you spend it *wisely*. Your foremost concern should be with the clarity of the document—whether it gets the message across. Once you're satisfied with the clarity of your message, you can then start to edit with an eye toward brevity. Then, and only then—in my view,—should you begin to worry about how *interestingly* it reads. Sure, the ideas you're trying to get across might very well be more compellingly expressed with a more original set of words or with a clever analogy. The question, though, is whether you can afford the time it takes to come up with original words and clever analogies, and whether the improvement is worth the effort. Most people in business can't afford the time, and most improvements of this nature, in business at least, go unnoticed.

So, if you're like most people, you'll want to approach editing as if you were a surgeon in a field hospital. You're careful and you work hard, but you recognize your limitations. You're not looking for artistic perfection, only to patch up the holes that need the most work and to do the patching as quickly as possible.

5. Get feedback from others.

One of the most critical—but least recognized—
advantages that professional writers enjoy over nonprofessionals is in the editing help they receive from other people
—people, incidentally, who *specialize* in salvaging manuscripts.
Before most pieces of professional writing see the light of print,
they're edited by a vertitable army of specialists. As a businessperson or a student, you don't have that luxury (if luxury is
what you want to call it), but this isn't to say that you can't find
someone—a friend or colleague—to fill a similar role, in return
for which you could offer a similar service. You're not looking
necessarily for somebody to tell you how good or, heaven for-
bid, how bad your writing is. You simply want somebody to
read what you've written and then to tell you, in his or her own
words, what *they* think you're trying to get across.

6. Edit in short segments.

Editing can be extraordinarily tedious, particularly
if you're sick to death of the piece you're writing as it is, or if
the editing involves a good deal of highly technical material. To
combat the carelessness or the apathy that is the inevitable by-
product of tedium, try to do your editing in short but intense
sessions (no more than fifteen minutes) punctuated by brief
breaks.

7. Read the manuscript slowly and out loud.

One of the more reliable, if not infallible, methods of
determining how much editing is necessary is to read your material aloud. Do it slowly and whenever you find yourself trip-
ping over words and phrases, take a closer look. Chances are,
you've uncovered a section that could do with some editing.
Another suggestion: if you're proofing your own work, start

from the end and read it backwards. Once you stop reading for meaning, you stand a much better chance of spotting typos.

8. *Keep a good dictionary handy.*

Better still, keep a running list of words you frequently mishandle in a notebook or on a sheet of paper near your writing desk.

The Basic Tools of Editing

If I can't offer you a true *system* of editing, I can at least suggest some specific techniques that have proven useful to me and to my students. As it happens, there are dozens of techniques you can call upon as an editor to clarify, to tighten, and to enliven a piece of writing. For practical reasons, though, I'll confine my discussion to the techniques I consider the most versatile—versatile in the sense that they deliver the most meaningful improvement in relation to the effort they require.

As I did when I taught editing as a system, I've divided the techniques into three general categories: (1) techniques that will enhance the clarity of your writing; (2) techniques that will make your writing more concise; and (3) techniques that will make your writing more engaging and interesting. I still recommend that you edit in this general sequence—dealing with clarity first, moving on to brevity, and leaving the third category of techniques for last—but the techniques within each category don't have to be used in any particular sequence. Use them as you see fit, depending, upon the shape of the manuscript.

Editing for Clarity

First the bad news. No technique I know of will *assure* you that what reads clearly to you in your own writing will read that way to your readers, although there have been a few interesting attempts to develop such a technique.

One such technique is known as the Fog Index, which was introduced in the 1950s by a highly respected writing consultant named Robert Gunning. The Fog Index is a measure of relative reading difficulty, arrived at through a formula that takes into account two factors: the average number of words in each sentence and the number of words of three syllables per 100 words.

Some writing instructors swear by the Fog Index, but I'm not entirely sold on it. I grant you that the shorter you keep your sentences and smaller you make your words, the less confusion you're likely to produce in your writing. More often than not, however, foggy writing has less to do with lengthy sentences or polysyllabic words, and more to do with foggy thinking and the failure to stage and sequence ideas in reader-oriented fashion.

Now the good news. If you learn to use most of the techniques I've already covered—in particular, Umbrellaizing, Who-Do Writing, Signposting, and Looping Back—your writing should read clearly. Even so, in the final analysis, the clarity of your writing depends primarily on your state of mind: on how much responsibility you as a writer are willing to assume to assure a successful writing transaction, and how much of a priority you give to expressing your ideas as clearly and as simply—as opposed to how stylistically impressive—as you can manage. If I've learned anything about successful writers over the past ten years, it's that they almost never take clarity for granted. More important, successful writers are not nearly as worried as unsuccessful writers are about "talking down" to their readers. They know, as *you* should know, that you almost never hear readers—especially readers of business correspondence—complain that something was too "easy" to read.

Check Individual Paragraphs for Umbrellaizing

The most effective technique for evaluating the clarity of your writing is also, unfortunately, the most cumbersome and time-consuming to use, so I recommend it with some reluctance. The idea is to go through each of your paragraphs sentence by sentence, ask yourself what thought each individual sentence is conveying, and then ask yourself if the paragraph is effectively Umbrellaized. Try the technique with the following paragraph.

The principle behind the telephone is well established. It is that the intensity of electrical current can vary as precisely as the air varies in intensity during the production of sound. The telephone can be an attractive device, too. This means that by speaking into an electromagnetic transmitter and by listening through an electromagnetic receiver, you can carry on a conversation with somebody else miles away.

It's obvious that the third sentence doesn't belong in this paragraph. It's also obvious that most errors of this nature won't be as nakedly apparent. No matter. I've used this example simply to reinforce the principles discussed in Chapter 6, and I only recommend the technique if you think you really need it. On the other hand, it's not a bad idea now and then, whether you think you need it or not, to take one of your paragraphs at random and subject it to this little test. Think of it as an exercise in quality control.

Clarifying Indefinite Pronouns

One of the more rampant sources of ambiguity in everyday writing are indefinite pronouns whose referents (i.e., the person or thing the pronoun refers back to) are either misleading or unclear. If you read the following memo, a version which I use in my seminar, you'll see what I mean.

Date: May 6, 1876

Memorandum
To: D. Thomas
From: A. T. Tee
Subject: Alexander Graham Bell Proposal

A new device with enormous commercial potential has been invented by a well-respected voice physiologist named Alexander Graham Bell. The device is known as the telephone, and Mr. Bell has proposed that we adopt and market it. He is awaiting our response, and I am recommending that we move quickly and accept the conditions in it.

The principle behind this is one that is well established. It is that the intensity of electrical current can vary as precisely as the air varies in intensity during the production of sound. This means that by speaking into an electromagnetic transmitter and by listening through an electromagnetic receiver, you can carry on a conversation with somebody else miles away.

The practical appeal of the telephone is obvious. Indeed a market survey has shown that 97% of Americans would purchase telephone service, if given the opportunity.

Mr. Bell has made two requests. One, he would like the outdoor structures being built for it to be named after the Actor Edwin Booth. Two, with respect to Don Ameche, he would like a movie to be made about his life.

Neither of these appears unreasonable, and both fall within previous licensing arrangements. It should prove to be one best product adoptions in our history, and I am urging that we accept it.

Notice that the sentences in this memo are short, and that the language is far from polysyllabic. Low Fog Index. Yet, the memo is anything but easy to read. That's because I've stacked it with indefinite pronouns lacking clear referents. As the writer, of course, *I* already know what the referents are. You, as the reader, *don't*.

Because this (excuse me, this *problem*) of indefinite pronouns is so common, I recommend to students that they take an almost ritualistic approach to the search for indefinite pronouns. One way to expedite this search is to circle *all* the indefinite pronouns on a page, without worrying at the time you circle whether or not the referents are clear. Here's how the memo might look if you followed this procedure.

Date: May 6, 1876

Memorandum
To: D. Thomas
From: A. T. Tee
Subject: Alexander Graham Bell Proposal

A new device with enormous commercial potential has been invented by a well-respected voice physiologist named Alexander Graham Bell. The device is known as the telephone, and Mr. Bell has proposed that we adopt and market (it.) He is awaiting our response, and I am recommending that we move quickly and accept the conditions in (it.)

The principle behind (this) is well established. The intensity of electrical current can vary as precisely as the air varies (in) intensity during the production of sound. Practically speaking, (this) means that by speaking into an electromagnetic transmitter and by listening through an electromagnetic receiver, you can carry on a conversation with somebody else miles away.

The practical appeal of the telephone is obvious. Indeed a market survey has shown that 97% of Americans would purchase telephone service, if given the opportunity.

Mr. Bell has made two requests. One, he would like the outdoor structures being built for (it) to be named after the actor Edwin Booth. Two, with respect to Don Ameche, (he) would like a movie to be made about (his) life.

Neither of (these) appears unreasonable, and both fall within previous licensing arrangements. (It) should prove to be one best product adoptions in our history, and I am urging that we accept (it.)

It isn't *essential* to circle indefinite pronouns in this way. I just think it simplifies the process. Once you've completed the circling, you take each circled pronoun, one at a time, and you ask yourself a simple question: is the referent obvious?

Let's ask ourselves this question in connection with the pronouns circled above.

The *it* that appears in the second sentence passes the test because we have no trouble connecting *it* to *telephone.* So, too, the *he* in the final sentence of that paragraph. The referent is clearly *Mr. Bell.*

Not so, however, the *it* that appears in the third sentence of the first paragraph? Does *it* loop back to *response, telephone,* or *proposal?* Tough to tell at first reading. To rectify the ambiguity, we need to replace *it* with *the proposal.*

Look at *this* in the first sentence of the second paragraph. Here, again, we're not sure what the referent is. We need to replace *this* with *the telephone.* The *this* in the third sentence could be replaced by *this relationship.*

Look at the fourth paragraph. Can you tell, as the paragraph is written, who, in fact, the movie is to be about? Not unless we specify that the movie is to be *about* Bell and that it is to *star* Don Ameche.

By making similar changes throughout the memo—supplying the referents whenever there is ambiguity—we produce a memo that now looks like this:

Date: May 6, 1876

Memorandum
To: D. Thomas
From: A. T. Tee
Subject: Alexander Graham Bell Proposal

A new device with a great commercial potential has been invented by a well-respected voice physiologist named Alexander Graham Bell. The device is known as the telephone, and Mr. Bell has proposed that we adopt and market it. He is awaiting our response, and I am recommending that we move quickly and accept the conditions in the proposal.

The principle behind the telephone is well established. The intensity of electrical current can vary as precisely as the intensity of air varies during production of sound. Practically speaking, this means that by speaking into an electromagnetic transmitter and by listening through an electromagnetic receiver, you can carry on a conversation with somebody else miles away.

The practical appeal of the telephone is obvious. Indeed a market survey has shown that 97% of Americans would purchase telephone service, if given the opportunity.

Mr. Bell has made two requests. One, he would like the outdoor structures being built for the invention to be named after the actor Edwin Booth. Two, Bell would like to see a movie made about his life, with Don Ameche in the lead role.

Neither of these requests appears unreasonable and both fall within previous licensing arrangements. The telephone should prove to be one of the best product adoptions in our history, and I am urging that we accept Mr. Bell's proposal.

Supply a "Who" to Subordinate Clauses

Subordinate clauses (clauses that modify the principal idea of a sentence) are often necessary, not only for emphasis and clarity but for variety as well. But such clauses, if used carelessly, produce ambiguity. Look at the following paragraph:

A new device with an enormous amount of commercial potential has been invented by a well-respected and eminent voice physiologist by the name of Alexander Graham Bell. Known as the telephone, a proposal has been submitted to us by Mr. Bell that we be the adopters and the marketers of it.

The problem here, of course, is that it isn't the *proposal* that is known as the *telephone*. Here's another example of the same mistake:

Highly marketable, I'm recommending that we accept the proposal as quickly as possible.

As written, it looks as if the writer is describing himself as *highly marketable.* The correction:

The telephone seems highly marketable, and I'm recommending that we accept the proposal as quickly as possible.

There are two ways to keep subordinate clauses from mucking up your writing. One way is to scrutinize with extra care any sentence that contains such clauses. The other—and perhaps more efficient—way is to keep your writing so simple that you won't be using many subordinate clauses to begin with. No snickering, please. More than a few good writers— Thoreau and Hemingway, to name two—never went out of their way to use subordinate clauses, and they are no less celebrated because of it.

Shorten Lengthy Sentences

My reservations about the Fog Index notwithstanding, lengthy sentences do tend to breed confusion and ambiguity. For this reason, shortening sentences is often an effective technique for enhancing clarity, especially in technical writing. Look at the following sentence:

The principle behind the telephone is well established in that the intensity of electrical current can vary as precisely as the air varies in intensity during the production of sound, meaning that by speaking into an electromagnetic transmitter and by listening through an electromagnetic receiver, you can carry on a conversation with somebody else miles away.

This sentence is not only *long,* it's confusing. It cries out for shortening.

The principle behind the telephone is well established. The intensity of electrical current can vary as precisely as the air varies in intensity during the production of sound. Practically speaking, this means that by speaking into an electromagnetic transmitter and by listening through an electromagnetic receiver, you can carry on a conversation with somebody else miles away.

Notice where we've made the breaks: at the *logical* points in the longer sentence, where one thought ends and another begins.

Here's another example:

The practical appeal of the telephone is obvious inasmuch as a recent market survey has shown that 97% of Americans would purchase it, if given the opportunity.

The revision:

The practical appeal of the telephone is obvious. A recent market survey has shown that 97% of Americans would purchase it if given the opportunity.

Editing for Brevity

The virtues of brevity in writing speak for themselves. The leaner and the more concise your writing, the more likely it is to read clearly and have a strong impact. Brevity is particularly cherished in business correspondence. Nobody, as I suggested earlier, reads business correspondence for the pure pleasure of it.

Each of the techniques in this section is designed to produce the same result: to cut the excess verbiage—the fat—from your sentences. Before you slip into your surgical gown, however, a brief lecture on brevity.

First of all, bear in mind that brevity isn't necessarily measured by how much space the writing occupies on a page, but by how long it takes your readers to navigate that space. Often, in fact, the most effective way to streamline a memo or report isn't to go at it with a scalpel but to alter the *format* of the piece: to break long passages into shorter paragraphs, to list information bullet-style, or to widen the margins so that there is plenty of white space around the borders.

You also want to be careful that in your zeal to slice the fat from sentences you don't cut into bone and thereby compromise clarity. Deleting a vivid example of a point you've made with a general statement could indeed reduce a paragraph by, say, twenty percent, but it could also leave the reader with a weaker conception of the point you're trying to make. It's a trade-off I don't recommend.

The point, then, is that while less *is* usually more in writing, there will still be times when, not only for the sake of clarity and emphasis but sometimes for the sake of internal politics or simple tact, you'll want to deliberately stretch a thought that could have been expressed in one sentence into three or four sentences. The sentence, "Your application has been rejected," may be concise and to the point, but certainly is not the most sensitive way to inform a job candidate she's not right for the job. By the same token, it's being courteous, not wordy, to explain that while you are impressed with her qualifications there simply aren't any openings in your company right now, but that you'll be keeping her resume on file. Such a courteous approach also makes good business sense.

With these caveats in mind, let's examine a few of the best ways to tighten up your writing style.

Eliminate Redundancy

Redundant words or phrases—sometimes referred to as tautologies—are words or phrases that do nothing but take up room in your sentences. You're being redundant when you describe yourself as a *non-paid volunteer,* when you seek a *temporary loan,* when you *tentatively suggest* to someone that they should do more *advance planning,* or when you explain that your company believes in *training in order to equip people to do their jobs effectively.*

Redundancy is a simple enough principle to understand, but redundancies themselves can be devilishly difficult to uncover in your writing. That's because most of us use redundancies so routinely in our everyday speech that when they crop up in our writing, we pay them no mind. They're part of our linguistic furniture. Look at the following list and ask yourself how many of these or similar phrases would crop up if you were to tape-record your own day-to-day conversations:

- firm commitment
- new innovation
- the most unique
- glance briefly
- true facts
- personal friend
- loud clamor
- painful ache
- lively excitement
- the reason is because

The bigger problem with redundancies, though, is that one can't always tell whether a word is in fact necessary to assure the right meaning or produce the proper emphasis. It depends on the situation and the objective. Here's an example of a sentence in which some of words and phrases are obviously redundant while others are less so.

A new device with an enormous amount of commercial potential has been invented by Alexander Graham Bell, a well-respected and eminent voice physiologist.

Stripped to its essentials, this sentence would read as follows:

A device has been invented by Alexander Graham Bell.

The stripped–down version is clear and concise, but it doesn't produce much impact. Nor does it accomplish the objective of the sentence, which is to drum up some excitement for this terrific new invention. So let's look at the sentence phrase by phrase and see what should be cut and what should be kept:

1. *new device:* Problematical. You could argue that "invented" *implies* "new," but I think *new* gives the phrase a needed sense of importance. I would keep it.

2. *with an enormous amount of commercial potential:* The idea here—that there is commercial potential in this device—is important. So, I submit, is the fact that the commercial potential is *enormous.* What we don't need, however, is *amount of,* or *an.*

3. *a well-respected and eminent voice physiologist:* It's important to give Bell credibility, but since *well respected* and *eminent* mean pretty much the same thing, we don't need both. Choose one or the other.

Once we make these cuts, the sentence reads as follows:

A new device with enormous commercial potential has been invented by Alexander Graham Bell, a well-respected voice physiologist.

Let's look at another example:

A recent market survey conducted not long ago has shown the result that 97% of Americans would purchase telephone service if given the opportunity to do so.

There's not much debate here since the sentence is laced with redundancies. You don't need both *recent* and *not long ago:* either works well as a solo. Nor do you need *the result;* it's more than implied by *has shown.* Finally, you don't need *to do so.* The revision:

A recent market survey has shown that 97% of Americans would purchase telephone service if given the opportunity.

If there is one faculty needed above all others to weed out the redundancies in your writing, it's mental alertness—that and the energetic resolve to comb every sentence you edit with the tenacity of a customs officer convinced there's contraband somewhere in the flight bag he's examining. There's no other way. You have to suspect *every* sentence as a potential harborer of redundancy. You need to look at every word and ask yourself, "Is this word really needed? Would the sentence work as well without it?"

As you conduct your search, be particularly suspicious of adjectives and adverbs and be wary of prepositional phrases, especially when you find two or three of them bunched together. Some examples to prove my point:

Instead of:

Mr. Bell has requested that the exterior outdoor structures being built for the telephone be named after the memory of the late actor Edwin Booth.

this:

Mr. Bell has requested that the outdoor structures being built for the telephone be named after actor Edwin Booth.

Instead of:

Neither of these requests appears unreasonable and both fall within the framework of the realm of previous licensing arrangements.

this:

Neither of these requests appears unreasonable and both fall within previous licensing arrangements.

Release Closet Verbs

Closet Verb is the term I use to describe action verbs that lie buried inside bulky noun phrases. In the phrase *we are engaged in the discussion,* for example, there is an action verb—*discuss*—buried inside the noun *discussion.* Take that verb *out* of the noun—we no longer need *engaged in the,* we simply write *discussing.*

Closet Verbs, sometimes known as concept nouns, are favored by people who labor under the regrettable delusion that when you take a simple verb and *nominalize* it—i.e., turn it into a noun phrase—you imbue your writing with added authority and dignity. You don't. The only thing Closet Verbs do for your writing style is to fill it with hot air. So it's fortunate that

Closet Verbs are relatively easy to edit out of your writing. They nearly always end in a suffix like *-tion, -ence,* or *-ance,* and are usually followed by *that* or by a preposition, usually *in* or *of.* Here are some typical examples:

Instead of:

The telephone has the appearance of such great marketability.

this:

The telephone appears highly marketable.

Instead of:

I am making the recommendation that we make a move quickly, and accept the proposal.

this:

I recommend that we move quickly and accept the proposal as quickly as possible.

Instead of:

Mr. Bell would like us to be the adopters and marketers of it.

this:

Mr. Bell would like us to adopt and market it.

Favor the Active Voice over the Passive

As I pointed out in Chapter 7, the passive voice, so prevalent in heavy-handed bureaucratic prose, won't be a problem for you if you learn to write Who-Do style. But should passive constructions sneak through during your revisions, they present you with good opportunities for cutting during editing. Turning passive constructions into the active voice nearly always shortens your sentences.

Instead of:

A request has been made by Mr. Bell that the outdoor structures being built for the telephone be named after the actor Edwin Booth.

this:

Mr. Bell has requested that the outdoor structures being built for the telephone be named after the actor Edwin Booth.

Or:

Mr. Bell has requested that we name the outdoor structures being built for the telephone after the actor Edwin Booth.

Instead of:

It has been proposed by Mr. Bell that we adopt and market the telephone.

this:

Mr. Bell has proposed that we adopt and market the telephone.

Editing Beyond Clarity and Brevity

I was tempted briefly to leave out this section of the editing chapter, not because there aren't several editing techniques that go beyond editing for clarity and brevity, but because most everyday writing doesn't require you to edit with this added dimension of sophistication. Mind you, I didn't say most writing couldn't *use* it. I said it wasn't *required*.

Consider the previous paragraph. Had I wanted to, I could have expressed the same ideas in that paragraph in an almost infinite number of ways. Instead of using *tempted,* I could have used the more colloquial phrase, *toyed with the idea.* Instead of linking the two sentences, as I did, I could have put a period after *chapter* and started the next sentence with the phrase *This is.* I didn't really *need* the phrase *Mind you,* but I prefer to write conversationally and so I use phrases like *mind you* often.

The problem, then, is where to draw the line—where an editing "technique" becomes simply a matter of personal taste. I'm not sure I have the answer, but none of the techniques I've included in this section is particularly esoteric, and all of them should prove useful in your everyday writing.

Getting Around the He/She Dilemma

Certain types of writing—instructional writing, for instance—put you into what I often call the He/She bind. The dilemma is whether to use the pronoun *he* or *him* when referring to both men and women and risk being labeled a sexist, or to use a *he/she* or *him/her* construction and risk being labeled a stilted writer.

Happily, there are several ways of getting around this dilemma. Here are the three most practical:

1. *Pluralize, where possible.*

This is probably the easiest technique to use when you want to get around *he/she.* You simply pluralize the subject and replace the *he* or *she* with *they* or *their.*

Instead of:

An employee who wants to change his work schedule should make any changes known by Tuesday, at noon.

this:

Employees who want to change their work schedules should make any changes known by Tuesday, at noon.

2. *Revise to eliminate the pronoun.*

Instead of:

An employee who wants to change his work schedule should make his changes known by Tuesday, at noon.

this:

Employees should make known any desired schedule changes by Tuesday, at noon.

3. *Use you, when appropriate.*

Instead of:

Our program gives each student a chance to pursue his particular career goals.

this:

Our program gives you a chance to pursue your particular career goals.

Warming Up Your Writing Style

If your writing consists mainly of technical reports or memos whose sole purpose is to convey information, you probably don't have to worry about how people respond personally to your writing. In most writing situations, on the other hand, especially those in which you'd like a favorable response from your readers, the ground rules change. Compare the following letters:

April 20, 1985

Thurgood E. Baker
Sales Manager
Pie-in-Sky Products
499 Fortune Ave.
Atlanta, Ga.

Dear Mr. Baker:

This letter is to confirm the arrangements made on the phone this morning for the shooting of a left-handed screwdriver demonstration film for the Pie-in-Sky sales force.

The shooting is scheduled to begin on Wednesday, May 1 at 9:30 A.M. and the cooperation of the training department supervisors is desired.

Every attempt will be made to keep to a minimum disruption that can be expected to occur during the shooting. Special portable equipment is being used and the setting up, the shooting, and the clearing up of equipment should take no more than four hours.

Attached herewith are permission forms. These must be signed by each supervisor who will be appearing in the film.

If it can be arranged, kindly remit the forms as soon as possible.

Sincerely yours,

Harry Nelson
President, Fly-By-Night Productions, Inc.

* * *

April 20, 1985

Thurgood E. Baker
Sales Manager
Pie-in-Sky Products
499 Fortune Ave.
Atlanta, Ga.

Dear Mr. Baker:

I enjoyed our conversation this morning and I'm writing to confirm the technical arrangements for the left-handed screwdriver demonstration film we are shooting for the Pie-in-Sky sales force.

We're scheduled to shoot, as you know, on Wednesday, May 1, at 9:30 A.M., and we're going to need the cooperation of your training department. In particular, we're hoping that your training supervisors will be able to serve as demonstrators in the film.

We'll do our best, of course, to minimize the disruption. We'll be using special portable equipment and should be able to set up, finish shooting and clear out our equipment in less than four hours.

I've enclosed some permission forms. Would you be kind enough to have each supervisor who will be appearing in the film sign one and send the forms back to me as soon as possible?

Many thanks for your cooperation.

Sincerely yours,

Harry Nelson
President, Fly-By-Night Productions, Inc.

Both of these letters convey the same information, but the second is clearly the more readable. No surprise, either. The second is far more personal: it is literally flooded with personal pronouns.

Making more frequent use of personal pronouns in your writing seems easy enough to do on the surface, but some people find the technique inordinately difficult, as if using personal pronouns when they write violates some religious or legal code. The problem many people have with personal pronouns arises, I'm sure, from the fact that using these pronouns has long been discouraged in most school writing programs. Consider, however, the difference in the following examples:

Instead of:

This letter is to confirm our conversation today.

this:

I'm writing to confirm our conversation today.

Instead of:

Every attempt will be made to minimize disruption.

this:

We'll do our best to minimize disruption.

Instead of:

It has come to our attention.

this:

I just heard.

To appreciate even more what personal pronouns can do for your writing, compare the following two versions of portions of the same letter. In the first version, I've gone out of my way to *avoid* using personal pronouns. Notice how stiffly it reads as a result. The second and more personalized version was written by one of the country's top copywriters.

Dear Mr. Malone:

The most substantial portion of the typical person's net worth is *trapped.* The reason is the Equity in his or her home. That Equity—the difference between what is owed on a home and what the home is worth—belongs to the homeowner. Indeed, property values have sky-rocketed so much over the last decade in Fairfield County that people don't realize what a significant amount of money Equity really has become.

The fact of the matter is that many Fairfield County homeowners are letting their Equity go to waste. Rather than liberating their capital, they let it merely sit there. Yet, the truth is that this money is the homeowner's and the homeowner doesn't have to wait to sell his or her house to put that cash to work for him or her.

* * *

Dear Mr. Malone:

If you're at all typical, the most substantial portion of your net worth is trapped.

I'm talking about the Equity in your home. That Equity—the difference between what you owe on your home and what it's worth—is your money. Indeed, property values have skyrocketed so much over the last decade in Fairfield County that you may not even realize what a significant amount of money your Equity really has become.

The fact of the matter is that many Fairfield County homeowners are letting their Equity go to waste. Rather than liberating their capital, they let it merely sit there. Yet, the truth is that this is your money and you don't have to wait to sell your house to put that cash to work for you.

Use Paralleling for Smoother Flow

Paralleling is the name I give to a technique, used routinely by professionals but often shunned by novice writers, which consists of structuring several sentences in a paragraph or several phrases in the same sentence in a more or less parallel fashion. Here are two paragraphs, the first of which was written with a conscious effort to *vary* sentence structure, and the second of which employs the technique of Paralleling. Read each carefully and decide for yourself which one reads better.

We have discussed the situation with each of our suppliers. The extent of our problems has been described to them. Making our suppliers more aware of the extent of our problems has been one of our goals. They have been told of the advantages to them if they cooperate. Everything that can be done we are doing.

We have discussed the situation with each of our suppliers. We have described the extent of our problems and have done our best to make our suppliers understand what we require. We have also told them of the advantages to them if they cooperate with us. All things considered, we are doing everything we can do.

Paralleling is a useful technique when you're writing speeches (most of us never worry about varying sentence structure when we talk), and useful, too, when you have a lot of information that you want to get across quickly. Here's an example from an article about Pittsburgh I wrote not long ago for *U.S. Air* magazine.

Most people happening upon Pittsburgh for the first time are indeed surprised that the city doesn't quite jell with the stereotyped reputation it has lived with even before British novelist Anthony Trollope described the city, in 1862, as *the blackest place I ever saw.* People are surprised at how green everything is (assuming they come here during the early fall, spring, or summer) along the fourteen-mile stretch of suburbia that connects the Greater Pittsburgh Airport to downtown Pittsburgh. They are surprised, once they emerge from the Fort Pitt Tunnel, at the power, opulence, and the glitter of the Pittsburgh skyline, and, if they arrive at night, when the two rivers—the Allegheny and the Monongahela, which angle toward one another as they flow along the banks of Pittsburgh's downtown area into the Ohio River—are shimmering with the lights from the office towers above, they are surprised at the sheer drama of the panorama.

As you can see, I've jammed quite a bit information into this paragraph, and some of the sentences are long enough to jar the Fog Index. But because I've used similar phrases in almost every sentence—*people are surprised*—the material still flows smoothly. That's what Paralleling does for you: it steps up the *pace* of your writing but doesn't compromise clarity. Because the words arrive in more or less the same package, readers can absorb the information more easily and more rapidly.

Paralleling, of course, shouldn't be overused, and you'll notice that I've used some specific devices (a parenthetical phrase here, an italicized word there, and Signposts sprinkled throughout) to prevent the rhythm that Paralleling can produce from becoming too monotonous.

In general, though, I find that Paralleling is *underused* in most business writing. A typical business paragraph, for example, might read as follows:

The new system allows the user to tailor its office filing and document handling through the use of shared files. There is no limit to the number of file cabinets assigned to individual users. Assignments are given automatically to each user.

There are three sentences here, each with a *different* sentence structure. Consider the revision:

The new system allows the user to tailor its office filing and document handling through the use of shared files. It places no limits on the number of file cabinets assigned to individual users, and it gives assignments to each user automatically.

Nothing fancy here. Since we want to follow a parallel pattern, we must use the same Who-Do pattern that was used in the first sentence. So we begin with the Who *(It)* and supply a Do *(places no limits)*. We do the same thing for the last sentence, adding the Signpost *and* to break the rhythm.

The information, of course, stays the same; the pattern changes, and with that change comes a noticeable improvement in readability.

11 | Making It Happen

I began this book by proposing that although writing may present cognitive challenges for which our neural circuitry isn't ideally suited, the writing process doesn't have to be as painful as most people find it. As you should appreciate by now, there are several steps you can take to reduce the pain. For openers, you can take a more realistic attitude to your writing and accept the fact that to be effective in your day-to-day writing you don't have to write like John Updike or Norman Mailer. You can also structure your schedule and organize your surroundings in ways more intelligently keyed to the demands of writing. And, finally, you can gradually begin to program into your writing approach certain basic writing patterns that will enable you to express your thoughts, more naturally, in a reader-oriented form.

In this chapter, I'd like to propose an actual "system" that will help you to integrate the concepts and techniques I've covered in this book into your own writing routine. Before I do this, however, let me issue a few disclaimers.

To begin with, don't take the word *system* too literally. No matter how systematic a writer you become, and no matter how faithfully you put into practice the recommendations I've been making throughout this book, certain aspects of the writing process will always remain outside your active control, and, except for the most routine tasks, writing will always oblige you to do a certain amount of groping in the dark. Accept it.

Sometimes, too, depending on the situation and the pressure you're under, you may have no option but to throw to the wolves everything I've tried to explain to you in this book and simply crunch your writing out the way you've crunched it out for most of your life.

Finally, the system I'm recommending will only work to the extent that you heed the advice I gave you earlier in the book about your attitude and the conditions in which you write. No system can overcome a self-defeating mental set or chaotic surroundings.

How to "Plan" a Writing Task

The first step to becoming a more systematic writer is to *plan* your writing more efficiently: that is, to approach each writing task (as much as possible) according to a logically thought-out schedule. I talked about the need to set aside blocks of time in Chapter 3, but here I'm talking about the need to plan each writing task within the framework of these blocks.

It's not as complicated as it may sound. The key is to figure out, as best you can, your normal writing pace—how long it usually takes to write the kinds of things you normally write—and then to plan a schedule related to that pace.

I know. The time it takes you to finish a writing task depends on what you're writing. It could be an hour; it could be a week. But I'm not asking you to come up with too specific a number, simply a ballpark idea of how long it takes you—once you've done all your research—to turn out a page of finished copy from first draft to final form.

A good way to arrive at this figure is to maintain a log during a period in which you're working on the kinds of writing tasks you normally handle. Keep track of the amount of time you spend writing from the moment you finish gathering your research until you've produced the finished document. (If you want to include research time, go ahead, but research in most cases will vary too much from situation to situation to give you a precise figure.) Once you've kept a log for three or four writing tasks, take the total number of manuscript pages you've completed during this time (figure double-spaced for uniformity), and divide by the number of hours you spent on the projects. The figure you end up with will represent your page rate per hour.

Is there an *average* page rate per hour? Who's to say? Most professionals I know say they're happy if they can turn out three or four *finished* pages in a day, which would break down to a page or so every two hours. Mary Lou Weisman, an accomplished essayist, says she's delighted if she can produce two or three good pages in a day, and Anatole Broyard, once he's thought about his material, says he can write a book review in about five or six hours, which breaks down roughly to about a page an hour.

My guess is that most people who write in business and professional situations should be able to average between one and two pages an hour, the figure varying, of course, according to the difficulty of the task and how "finished" the writing has to be. Brochure copy, for example, generally takes longer than routine memos. Proposals usually take longer than reports.

For the sake of argument, though, let's say that you find your own rate to be about one page every two hours. (Don't be depressed: at that rate, you could spend two hours a day writing and turn out a ninety-thousand-word novel in less than a year.) If this is the case, and you're working on a document that will be, say, six pages, you can figure a minimum of twelve hours of writing, not counting the time it may take you to gather your research.

Once you come up with this figure—the estimated number of hours it's going to take you to finish a writing task working at your normal pace—you're ready to map out a rough schedule. *How* you schedule your time is up to you. You might want to schedule six two-hour blocks, eight one and one-half-hour blocks, or twelve one-hour blocks; it doesn't matter, just as long as no block of time is *less* than an hour.

What *does* matter is that you give yourself sufficient time to complete each stage of the process: to plan, to get your first draft on paper, to revise, and to edit. Here's a sample plan you might want to follow:

Stage I: Planning (approximately 25 percent of estimated time)

During this stage, you complete your Envisioning Chart (in particular the Target Statement), take command of your material (reading your notes over and over again), work with a Satellite Outline, organize your material, and, if you like, do some freewriting.

Stage II: Composing and Revising (approximately 60 percent of estimated time)

You could begin this stage with freewriting, or by using some of the techniques we've covered in this book (ORSON, Umbrellaizing, Who-Do Writing) to produce a first draft and perhaps two or three revisions, depending upon how you like to write. You might also find it useful during this stage of the process to devote individual sessions to working on individual sections of your document. Your goal, in any case, is to produce a draft in reasonably finished form.

Stage III: Proofreading and Editing (approximately 15 percent of estimated time)

Proofreading and editing should begin only when you're satisfied that you've produced a reasonably finished draft, and should be done in short bursts of intense concentration.

I submit this plan only as a suggestion, and I invite you to vary it any way you see fit. On some projects, for instance, it might make more sense to spend 30 percent or 40 percent of your overall time in the planning stages and less time on the composing, revising, and editing. You'll have to experiment to find out what proportion works best for you. But let me stress two principles that apply regardless of how you vary the proportions.

First, try to allow some time—a day at least—between the planning stage (organizing, etc.) and the first day you intend to put words to paper. The idea is to give all the thinking you've done a chance to germinate and take root in your mind. It always helps my writing the next morning, I know, if I go to bed with my general plans and strategy percolating in my mind.

Second, try to adhere to the schedule you set for yourself. If you find yourself falling behind, readjust the schedule. The point is to stay in control of your time.

Managing the Act

Other than to have you review the techniques I've covered in earlier chapters, there isn't too much I can suggest to help you achieve fluency *while* you're writing. No one can climb inside your brain and *execute* for you. What I *can* offer, though, are four very general suggestions that have proven helpful to me, and to other writers I know, from time to time.

1. *Focus on objectives and thoughts, not words.*

Writing, as I've been preaching all long, involves far more than simply choosing words. Writing is establishing objectives, planning a strategy, and expressing thoughts in patterns that meet the needs of readers. The more intelligently you sequence these decisions, the more you reduce the range of choices that need to be made at any stage of the process and the less strain it takes to make the best choice. Once you know what you want to accomplish, you narrow the range of options to only those approaches capable of achieving your objective. Once you've determined, in general, what you must do to stimulate interest, guarantee understanding, gain acceptance, and produce motivation, you further limit the range of thought options. Once you've figured out the thought options, you reduce the range of words and groups of words that must be produced to represent the thoughts. Finally, once you've programmed in your mind specific patterns that deliver those words in a reader-oriented form, you've reduced the range of options even further.

I don't mean to make it all sound as simple as snapping together the parts of a plastic model airplane. It's not. Your options at any stage of the sequence aren't *eliminated,* they're simply reduced. You still have to make choices. I'm convinced, though, that the logic of this approach is sound. I know, for example, that when I'm having trouble coming up with the right words for an article or even a letter, it usually means that I'm not sure of what thoughts I want to get across, and it's a sign that I need to take a step back and try to get a clearer fix on the ideas I'm trying to get across. And when I'm having trouble with specific thoughts, it's a safe bet that I'm in too much of a hurry and haven't doped out my strategy clearly enough. Recognizing my folly doesn't *solve* the problem, of course, but it generally gets me moving again. I don't spend as much time as I used to staring at empty pages.

2. *Speak it as you write it.*

If you're not already doing it, get into the habit of saying aloud each word as you write it. Then, if you find yourself stuck, go back and repeat sentences you've already written and let the natural rhythm of your thoughts produce the words. What "writing aloud" seems to do, for reasons I can't explain, is to get the words out of your head more quickly than they seem to come when you write in silence. Writing aloud also helps to keep your mind from drifting and will help, in the long run, to develop your "ear." You'll discover that when the writing doesn't "sound" smooth, it's not likely to read smoothly, either. I can't remember when I picked up the habit of talking aloud as I write, but I can't remember ever *not* doing it. I'm so used to it, it's impossible for me *not* to talk to myself when I write.

3. *Vary the nature of the workload.*

The late Richard Gehman, an unusually facile and prolific magazine writer in the 1950s, always liked to work on several projects at once. His reasoning was that each stage of writing an article—the research, the organization, the first draft, the revising, etc.—calls for a different mental approach. So, when he was having trouble finding the handle during the first-draft of a piece, he'd switch to a piece that was nearly finished and do some editing.

If your writing consists primarily of short memos or letters or if you rarely work on more than one piece of writing at a time, Gehman's approach isn't likely to do you much good, but if your writing workload is such that you can vary the nature of your writing tasks from day to day, give the idea some thought. If nothing else, working on a variety of writing projects at the same time helps prevent one of the most common, if overlooked, sources of blocking: boredom. It's possible to become bored—"dulled" might be a better way of putting it— regardless of how interesting the project may be. But if you can move back and forth among projects—perhaps work on two or three in a day—you'll never run into that problem. Yes, you sometimes have trouble recapturing a certain train of thought when you leave a project, work on something else, and then come back again. But, in and of itself, moving from project to project has a way of keeping your mind alert.

4. *Write in Portions.*

One of the nice things about writing, as opposed to speaking, is that you can produce the information in any order you choose. Nobody who reads your finished report or memo cares if you wrote the last sentence first, or started in the middle, or wrote the conclusion before you finished the introduction. (And, by the way, starting with your conclusion is often the best way to begin a complicated writing task: knowing where you want to end up has an uncanny way of clarifying your focus.)

The point is, fight the tendency to just sit there and staring at a blank page and allowing the enormity of the task to overwhelm and depress you. Start somewhere. Anywhere. Set a small goal for yourself: a paragraph or two from the middle section, to be finished within the next hour. Set another goal: another paragraph or two. Keep in mind that ideas, once you've put them down on paper, often generate other ideas. And keep in mind, too, that when you put together a series of well-constructed sections, you end up with a well-constructed whole.

5. *Pace yourself.*

Your brain is a thinking machine, not a muscle, but it is similar to your muscles in one crucial respect: it can work efficiently for only so long, and then it starts to lose its edge. Unfortunately, it's easier to tell when your muscles are tired than it is to tell when your brain needs a rest, and that's why the condition known as burnout has become so prevalent in our society. Most people aren't aware of how overworked their brains are until they wake up one morning and find themselves unable to concentrate on anything for more than two or three seconds.

Writing taxes your brain's resources as much as any activity I can think of. All things considered, the brain can hack the challenge, but it has its limitations and you need to respect them. You need to be energized when you write, but you also need to stay relaxed enough to keep the juggling act under reasonable control and maintain the perspective necessary to produce reader-oriented writing. It's a tricky balance no matter how long you've been doing it, but it's a balance you need to learn to maintain, regardless of the pressure you may be under.

Let me tell what I've recently begun to do. When I'm up against a deadline, I organize my writing schedule around a certain number of blocks of time per day, each block consisting of between forty-five minutes to fifty minutes, with a ten- or fifteen-minute break in between. I have a small timer, which I set for forty-five-minute intervals, and when the bell rings I finish up whatever sentence I'm working on and take a break. I'll do some stretching, go through my mail, clean up my desk, make a phone call or two, get some coffee, or walk outside to get some air. I take this break, it's worth pointing out, even if I'm moving along at a good clip. Experience has assured me that if I get back to my work within ten or fifteen minutes, I can generally begin at the same pace.

Writing in *planned* blocks of time like this works well for me for several reasons. First of all, I'm more efficient. I don't get sidetracked as easily as I used to get when my schedule was more random and I would write until I felt I *needed* a break. When it occurs to me as I'm writing (and you're always thinking odd little things as you write) that I have to get in touch with somebody or tend to some detail—like making an appointment to get the car serviced—the itch to get this detail off my mind doesn't interfere with my concentration. I simply jot it down, knowing that I'll tend to it during my next break, which is never more than forty-five minutes away. I find, too, that when people call, I'm not as tempted as I used to be to take care of the call at that minute. I simply tell my callers I'll get back to them within the hour.

Writing Blocks and What to Do About Them

If you had dropped by my office at about eleven o'clock one recent morning, you would have found me vacuuming the carpet. Not that the carpet was in *need* of vacuuming: it was actually fairly clean. The problem, though, was that I was having an inordinate amount of trouble with a section of this book. So, what I was doing wasn't vacuuming the carpet. What I was doing was avoiding writing.

Vacuuming a carpet isn't the only way I avoid writing. I sometimes avoid writing by straightening out my desk, by emptying the wastebasket, by getting a cup of coffee from the kitchen, by taking an empty coffee cup *back* to the kitchen, by sharpening pencils (even though I use a word processor), by changing the radio station because I'm tired of listening to classical music, or by changing the radio station because I *want* to listen to classical music.

The phenomenon I'm talking about is usually referred to as a writer's "block," and as I mentioned in Chapter 2, it is something that nearly everyone who writes runs into every now and then. Blocks frequently occur when you first sit down to write, but they can strike at any time or at any stage in a writing project and they can produce varying degrees of paralysis. Some writers I know say they've never been blocked for more than a few hours at a time, but I know of writers who've been blocked so severely they've gone to psychiatrists. I know of one fairly well-known writer, who, after writing a best-seller in the late 1950s, had so much trouble getting started on her second book (it eventually came out about ten years later), she sued her interior decorator. Her contention was that the decorator's incompetence had caused her so much aggravation, she was unable to complete the book.

Getting to the Root of the Problem

What, exactly, *are* writing blocks? Why do they occur? Why are certain writers more susceptible to them than others, and why is blocking more likely to occur on certain kinds of writing projects than others?

These are all reasonable questions, but they are not simple questions to answer. To begin with, it's not easy to distinguish a true block from the difficulty *inherent* in writing. It could be argued, as I mentioned in the Introduction, that when you're writing something complicated or highly personal, getting your ideas to flow freely from mind to paper is not meant to be painless. Gay Talese says he can sometimes spend a day working on just two or three paragraphs, not because he's blocked, but because he's refining the language or, as he likes to put it, "choreographing" the flow. Betsy Weinstock observes that when the writing comes too easily to her, it often turns out to be not nearly as good as when she has to struggle with it. And Anatole Broyard, normally a fluid writer when he's writing articles or reviews, finds the going considerably slower when he's working on fiction, and the difficulty neither surprises nor disturbs him. "In fiction," he explains, "you're often struggling to find something that may be still locked in your consciousness."

Then, too, a block may be rooted in nothing more complicated than the way you happen to feel, physically or mentally, on a particular day. Maybe you didn't get to bed the night before until three A.M., or you have a touch of the flu, or you've just received a phone call from your accountant who has told you the IRS has been posing worrisome inquiries. Sometimes the problem may be purely technical: you simply haven't gathered enough information, or haven't spent enough time to take command of your information; you're simply not *ready* to write.

All the same, there do seem to be writing blocks that can't be explained by fatigue, or illness, or financial concerns, or a lack of preparation. I know because I've worked with students and businesspeople who, no matter *how* they feel, or *what* is on their minds, or how familiar they are with their material, are unable to write even the simplest of correspondence without blocking—and not because they're lacking in writing skills, either.

Exactly what happens in these cases to interfere with the flow of thoughts is anybody's guess. In rare cases, I suspect there is minimal brain dysfunction: a neurophysiological glitch that disrupts whatever "sorting" or "selection" process has to occur to produce an orderly flow of thoughts to paper. More often, however, I think a lot of people simply "choke" when they write; they become so intimidated by the pressure of having to meet a certain standard (their own or someone else's) that the circuits that control the process simply freeze.

Superficially, there's an easy enough solution to this problem: you simply learn to relax more; you stop caring about the outcome. This is the crux of the advice given to athletes for whom choking is a persistent problem. "Don't worry about whether you're going to win or lose," one sports psychologist I know counsels the groups of athletes he lectures. "Focus on something—the seams of the ball, for instance—that will get your mind *off* the outcome."

This technique is called "purposeful distraction," or, as Timothy Gallwey, author of *The Inner Game of Tennis,* refers to it, "stilling the mind." I've tried the technique on the tennis court on occasion and I must report that it works—if only to a point. But if you're going to try this when you write, you're faced with an obstacle unique to writing: stilling the very instrument—your mind—you need to work with in order to perform.

Probably the best way to deal with blocks is to take *preemptive* action: to establish a routine and to sequence your thinking in such a way that blocks are unlikely to occur. If you take to heart the advice embodied throughout this book—routinizing your environment, taking the time to assimilate your material, freewriting, working in patterns—all of these steps should go a long way to minimize, if not eliminate, blocking. But the most important thing to remember if you want to avoid blocking is to separate as much as you can the generative aspect of writing from the editing aspect of the process. The technique that will allow you to do this, of course, is freewriting—allowing your thoughts to materialize on paper without any initial concern for how they are structured and what precise words you might be using to express the thoughts.

But in the event you've taken all the steps I've suggested to you throughout this book, and you've tried freewriting without success, and you're *still* blocking, here are some additional suggestions:

1. *Change the medium.*

Thoughts that aren't materializing on your writing pad, typewriter, or computer screen might just flow more easily if you were to first *talk* them out—perhaps to an understanding friend, or, just as useful, into a tape recorder. The idea, as in freewriting, is to keep talking, even if you find yourself rambling. Once you've been at it for about five minutes or so, play the tape back and see if you can find some thread that will put you back on track.

Using a tape recorder to ease the agony of writing the first draft worked exceptionally for a high-school principal I know. The system he eventually adopted was to wake up a half-hour or so early on days when he had a lengthy memo to write and then, as he was shaving, getting ready for breakfast, and driving to the school, simply speak all of his thoughts into a tape recorder. Once he reached school, he would have his secretary type up his ramblings. He would then prepare a Satellite Outline and put together a reasonably finished draft. The system may sound a little complicated, but it enabled him to reduce by a good 40 percent the amount of time he spent on his writing during the week.

2. Read for inspiration.

You should be keeping within arm's reach of your writing desk a file or a notebook that is filled with letters, articles, even memos written in a style that might serve you as a "prompt" or model when you're struggling to find your writing rhythm. This material could represent the best of your own efforts or could be the work of other writers.

I know that when I'm having trouble finding a writing rhythm, reading certain writers can often get me going. The writers I use for this purpose include Michael Korda, Nora Ephron, Frank Deford, and William Zinsser, all of whose styles are marked by exceptional fluidity. What seems to happen as I read these writers is that the rhythm and the energy of their writing activates something in my own mind and gets me going.

Betsy Weinstock has an interesting suggestion in this regard: put your thoughts down in the style of another writer. Her logic: by putting the words down through another voice, you often circumvent the block. "Once you get started," she says, "you can then revert back to your own style."

3. Change your environment.

When Stanley Englebardt runs into a temporary writing block, he goes out jogging, and in extreme situations he'll take a hot bath. Getting *away* from the actual writing environment, he says, usually helps to clarify his thinking. Other writers I know take different measures. Richard Chesnoff putters in his garden. Mary Lou Weisman sometimes does a load of wash. And when Davis Weinstock finds himself blocked, he goes outside in his driveway (even if there's snow on the ground) and starts shooting baskets. "I make myself stay out there until I make ten in a row," he says. "For some reason, having accomplished that makes the writing seem that much easier."

The rationale here is that sometimes you're blocked because you're too close to your material and you've lost the ability to make clear judgments. Anything, therefore, you can do to change the nature of the stimuli impinging on your brain—a walk, a shower, a move to another room—can sometimes shake things loose and give you the perspective you're lacking. It makes eminent sense when you've run into a mental roadblock to move away, relax for a moment, do some deep breathing, take a walk—all for the purposes of retrenching.

There is, however, a danger here: you could give up too soon. John Fuller, for instance, has found that he's able to work through most blocks simply by sitting there and working harder, but he may be an exception. I often find that if, when I'm getting absolutely nowhere with my writing, I go on some mindless errand or do a little housekeeping, I am usually much better prepared to write when I return.